Custer's Forgotten Black Soulmate

*His Special Relationship
with African-American
Eliza Denison Brown*

Also by this author

Nat Turner's Holy War To Destroy Slavery
America's Female Buffalo Soldier: Cathy Williams
Miller Cornfield at Antietam
Pickett's Charge
Death at the Little Bighorn
Barksdale's Charge
Storming Little Round Top
Exodus From The Alamo
Emily D. West and the "Yellow Rose of Texas" Myth
The South's Finest
George Washington's Surprise Attack
How The Irish Won The American Revolution
Why Custer Was Never Warned
The Alamo's Forgotten Defenders
Irish Confederates
God Help The Irish!
Burnside's Bridge
The Final Fury
Westerners In Gray
Alexander Hamilton's Revolution
The Confederacy's Fighting Chaplain
Cubans In The Confederacy
Forgotten Stonewall of the West
From Auction Block To Glory
The Important Role of the Irish in the American Revolution
The 1862 Plot to Kidnap Jefferson Davis.
Anne Bonny: The Infamous Female Pirate
America's Forgotten First War for Slavery and Genesis of The Alamo
For Honor, Country, and God: Los Niños Héroes
Targeting Abraham: The Forgotten 1865 Plot To Assassinate Lincoln
A New Look at the Buffalo Soldier Experience in Wartime Vol I:
Corporal David Fagen's Metamorphosis and Odyssey
Nanny's War to Destroy Slavery
The Irish at Gettysburg
Blacks in Gray Uniforms
Glory At Fort Wagner: The 54th Massachusetts Vol I
Martyred Lieutenant Sanité Bélair
Gran Toya: Founding Mother of Haiti
Claudette Colvin: Forgotten Mother of the Civil Rights Movement
Mulan and the Modern Controversy

Custer's Forgotten Black Soulmate

*His Special Relationship
with African American
Eliza Denison Brown*

Phillip Thomas Tucker, Ph.D.

ISBN: 9798571016827

PublishNation LLC
www.publishnation.net

Contents

Introduction   1

Chapter I: Escape From Slavery   59

Chapter II: Fury of The Civil War Years   98

Chapter III: The Great Plains and the Indian Wars   119

Chapter IV: Wartime Casual Sex and Custer   138

Chapter V: The Most Forgotten Sexual Dynamics   171

Epilogue   228

About the Author   234

Introduction

The very last words that Lieutenant Colonel George Armstrong Custer said before riding off with his 7th Cavalry troopers on one of his Indian Campaigns on the Northern Great Plains were not said to his wife. Custer's wife hailed from the town of Monroe, Michigan, where she had been the town's fairest maiden in her younger days.

Instead of having been directed at his wife, Custer's final words of comfort shouted from horseback were said to a young black woman and former slave, who he had long treated with a measure of rare respect and much like a Custer family member. Revealing a confident certitude in having placed his complete trust in this homespun ex-slave woman from Rappahannock County, Virginia, Custer yelled these final words of advice to Eliza Denison Brown, "Take Care of Libbie, Eliza." Eliza was her slave name and the name of Brown was gained when she married after the Civil War.

Clearly, when it came to the care of his beloved wife, Elizabeth Clift Bacon, who was a traditional army wife after having met and married her husband during the Civil War, when he was away, Custer placed great trust in the sage judgement of Eliza, who he had known since late July 1863. But this special connection between Custer and the ex-slave woman from Virginia was nothing new to anyone who had been around the native Ohioan during the campaigns of the Civil War or during his early years of service on the Great Plains.

Custer had been placing his trust and confidence in Eliza for years and during most of the Civil War in which he had emerged as one of the North's top heroes by aggressively leading his cavalrymen to one victory after another against the finest cavalry of the Army of Northern Virginia.

Like no other Union cavalry commander in blue during the war years, Custer's hard-hitting style and tactical aggressiveness on the battlefield had played a key role in turning the tide on the final day at Gettysburg during the dramatic cavalry showdown on the East Cavalry Field on July 3, 1863. Here, in the Army of the Potomac's rear, Custer and his Michigan cavalry had saved the day, when everything had been at stake. And he had been instrumental in forcing the surrender of Robert E. Lee's Army of Northern Virginia at Appomattox Country House on April 9, 1865.

But who was Eliza and why has her story been overlooked and ignored for so long if she had been a longtime meaningful player in the Custer story? After all of the many books written about Custer and especially about his tragic June 25, 1876 death at age 36 at the hands of Sioux and Cheyenne warriors at the Little Bighorn in the Montana Territory, why has she still remained a shadowy and obscure figure shrouded by mystery to this day, despite the prominent role that she played in the lives of Custer and Eliza during both the Civil War and the Indian Wars?

Because she was an African American and nothing more than a lowly former slave from the Old Dominion, Eliza has been largely forgotten by history and lost in the mists of time, which has long been the dismal fate of so many significant African Americans throughout the course of American history. Most important, what made Custer feel that he could repeatedly and completely trust his wife in Eliza's good care and place his faith in her good judgement over an extended period of time?

Most of all, what was the mysterious nature of this seemingly inexplicable relationship and unique bond that had existed for years between Custer and Eliza and why was it so strong in two wars that defined the essence of America? Ironically, these questions have never been asked or sufficiently answered by generations of historians, mostly white male, traditional, and conservative, who have chosen to ignore the longtime outsized influence of this ex-slave from Virginia on Custer, despite Eliza having played a key role in the lives of Custer and his wife for the better part of a decade and during the Civil War and the Indian Wars.

Ever since he went down fighting with his command of more than 200 troopers of his five 7th Cavalry companies along the Little Big Horn in the Montana Territory on the afternoon of June 25, 1876, the subject of George Armstrong Custer, the former "boy general" of the Civil War, has been an endless source of fascination to the American people in no small part because of the incomprehensibility of his tragic fate at the hands of so-called primitive barbarians of the Northern Great Plains in one of the most one-sided Indian successes during the course of American history.

Generation after generation since that fateful afternoon for Custer and his 7th Cavalry in the Little Bighorn River country, Americans have wondered how one of the greatest northern heroes of the Civil War and a survivor of countless battles and skirmishers against some of the best cavalry and infantry of Lee's Army of Northern Virginia could have possibly been vanquished with his entire five-company command and killed in the far-away Montana Territory on the Northern Great Plains.

The timing of this stunning disaster on a short afternoon in one of America's most remote areas on the continent resulted in a severe blow to the psyche of a confident American nation, which was prosperous and growing by leap and bounds, during its long-awaited Centennial Celebration year of 1876.

For the American people who were caught-up in celebrating the one hundred year anniversary of America's birth in Philadelphia, Pennsylvania, on July 4, 1776, the shock of a multitude of Great Plains warriors from nomadic societies of the Sioux and Cheyenne nations having so thoroughly defeated the elite 7th Cavalry troopers of a modern army was overwhelming to the American people like no other event in recent memory. A large part of the shock to America stemmed from the fact that a good many white soldiers had been wiped out by warriors of a darker color.

In the end, Custer became a classic example of a modern Greek tragedy performed on America's isolated frontier and played out in full on the high ground above the waters of the Little Bighorn River, when a cruel fate, the ever-capricious Gods of War, and hubris ordained the disaster that stunned the American nation. In this sense, the final showdown on the bloody afternoon of June 25 was America's own Greek tragedy in perfectly fulfilling the necessary cultural and psychological requirements, when Custer's fate was sealed by a cruel reckoning in Montana.

The much-romanticized Custer legend and enduring myth, especially the story of Custer's "Last Stand" that has become the subject of seemingly countless books, have long secured a lofty place in the American memory and consciousness. The Custer mystique has endured to this day because of the longtime fascination about this unprecedented disaster among the general public.

In consequence, no single American military man has been the subject of more books than George Armstrong Custer not only because of his outstanding successes on Civil War battlefields, but also for what happened in only a short period of time along the Little Bighorn, where he met his tragic fate in the cruelest of ways.

Not even General George Washington or President Abraham Lincoln have drawn more attention, if not obsessiveness, from generations of American writers and historians more consistently than Custer. Almost every American author has long portrayed Custer, already an anachronism in his own time although a fact never realized by him at the time, in the most favorable light and perspective.

Without exaggeration and even during the most inglorious of campaigns in battling a weaker people who were only defending their beloved Northern Great Plains homeland and nomadic way-of-life as a free people, Custer still maintained the badly-outdated image of the bold cavalier hero and romantic knight of a bygone age to the bitter end: all part of Custer's excessive glorification that had been begun by the northern media and public from his long list of successes that he reaped during the Civil War.

A seemingly endless cast of uncritical American historians, writers, and journalists, Custer himself in self-serving writings, and even his own wife in her own three books and articles have consistently presented the most romantic of images of Custer. And this endless process of romanticization and glorification has been especially the case in regard to the married couple's allegedly pure and pristine relationship enjoyed by Elizabeth and George, which has always been presented like something out of a best-selling romantic novel or fairy tale.

In her post-Little Bighorn trilogy, Elizabeth succeeded in creating the romantic illusion that Custer was a stainless saint in blue and the ideal husband, who served as the perfect model for Victorian Era men across the breath of America: an idolization that solidified Custer's hero status and enduring image.

But was this longtime portrayal of martial perfection actually the case in the Custer marriage as long emphasized by Elizabeth, who placed her dead husband on the loftiest of pedestals in her three books and articles that profoundly influenced a national audience for generations? And was this endless process of Custer's glorification based on facts or simply the typical romance of the Victorian Era? Again, these questions have been seldom asked by historians and still need to be addressed in greater detail at this late date.

Or was Custer's widow, who became the self-appointed guardian of her husband's saintly image for more than five decades after his tragic demise in the Montana Territory, only painting the most idealized of portraits of her dead husband for public consumption and to increase the sales of Elizabeth's books, which became so immensely popular to the general public? After all, her creation of the ideal romance and perfect hero-husband fueled book sales in the Victorian Era, when traditional values dominated American society and the concept of marriage was a holy one revered by society.

Conversely, in Elizabeth's prolific writings and in virtually all books about Custer to this day, Eliza Denison Brown has been depicted in an overall negative and demeaning way because of her color: the widely-accepted and seldom-questioned stereotypical view of blacks for generations of Americans in both the North and South.

Even Eliza's words from the penned conversations in Elizabeth's books were presented in a stereotypical way in keeping with how Victorian audiences expected a black person, especially a former slave, should speak and think very nearly in the Sambo traditions of the South. In Elizabeth's writings, Eliza has been portrayed in a way that conformed to the typical Deep South stereotypes of blacks of a negative nature, when she was a product of Rappahannock County in Northern Virginia and probably never picked cotton in her life.

Therefore, Elizabeth's own words played a role in reducing Eliza's overall image and status in the eyes of generations of historians, who have paid little attention to her in the Custer story because she was deemed so utterly insignificant by them. Such was not the case, however.

As the daughter of a respected judge, Elizabeth was raised in an environment of wealth and upper-class status of the privileged elite: the antithesis of the background and tragic world of Eliza, when she had come to age as a lowly slave without promise or expectations in the Virginia Piedmont.

In fact, Elizabeth hailed from a class—the upper crust of Monroe, Michigan—that was higher than that of her husband, who was from rural Ohio and was raised the son of a blacksmith. As could be expected, therefore, Elizabeth portrayed Eliza in a less than flattering light partly because she believed that she possessed the natural right and privilege to dictate to the former slave like a queen ruling a lowly subject, who was only meant to endlessly obey her every directive without question and beckon to her every whim: a natural development because Elizabeth and Eliza, who was intelligent and possessed a mind of her own, were typical products of two vastly different worlds that were entirely incomprehensible and incompatible to each other.

The cultural and societal gap that existed between the lives of Eliza and Elizabeth could not have been wider. And as in the normal course of events, the subservience of this hard-working ex-slave from Virginia was expected in every way by the pampered and spoiled blueblood from Monroe, because this was just a normal part of her aristocratic world of have's and have not's in Elizabeth's upper-class environment.

At this late date, virtually every aspect of Custer's life and legacy has been long explored and analyzed in great detail by legions of admiring historians, imaginative writers, and creative journalists and practically ever since the last shot at the Little Bighorn was fired in anger.

Therefore, seemingly everyone in the Custer story have become famous except for one who has been left unexplored and in dark obscurity to this day. And, ironically, this has been one of the most undeserved—certainly in the personal and private lives of Custer and his wife for an extended period—absences in the historical record of the Custer story only because this individual of African descent failed to conform with the romantic legend of Custer primarily because of her color and sex: the forgotten contributions and the overall importance of a humble young woman named Eliza Denison Brown and Custer's close relationship to her, which was more intimate on multiple levels than generally assumed by generations of historians.

After all, Brown was most likely of West African descent, because either her enslaved parents or grandparents had been forced to journey across the Atlantic during the infamous "Middle Passage" to reach America's shores. In consequence, any hint of the possibility of a close connection between the two—a lowly former slave and one of America's greatest war heroes--on any level except that of complete dominance and control maintained by Custer was practically unthinkable, because of Custer's lofty status. Most of all, the Custer-Eliza relationship has been a taboo subject in the Victorian Era and even in modern times.

Even more and for generations, this surprisingly close and intimate connection—the meeting of souls--between Custer and Eliza has been deliberately long ignored and overlooked because of the power of the Custer myth, which has long had a life of its own since his death at the Little Bighorn. Rumors about a sexual relationship between Custer and Eliza had long persisted among the men who served with Custer in both the Civil War and Indian Wars, including the troopers of his own 7th Cavalry.

Quite simply, this special and unique relationship between Custer and Eliza has been the most forgotten story behind the enduring myth and romantic legend of one of the greatest Northern heroes of the Civil War and one of the most iconic legends of America.

Most important and until the publication of this current book, a close look into the intimate nature of the forgotten Custer-Eliza relationship has not been previously undertaken by historians primarily because Eliza was black and long considered nothing more than a lowly camp cook and laundress, who has been seen as entirely unworthy to have been coupled with Custer in any way, shape, or form: not unlike the situation in which generations of American authors and historians have gone to great lengths for decades to deny the existence of intimate personal relationships that existed between famous Americans and black women--from Founding Father Thomas Jefferson of Virginia to anti-Civil Rights Senator Strom Thurmond of South Carolina.

Interestingly, in both cases, Jefferson and Thurmond, two powerful national politicians (Jefferson became the nation's third president beginning in 1801 and Thurmond campaigned for president in 1948) of Washington, D.C., began intimate relationships with women of color, Sally Hemings of Virginia and Essie Mae Washington of South Carolina, respectively.

These black women women worked for Jefferson and Thurmond as domestics in their private homes, just like Eliza long labored as a domestic worker (cook and laundress) close to Custer's presence for an extended period both before and after his early February 1864 marriage to Elizabeth.

However, generations of historians have underestimated the importance of Eliza and her outsized influence on multiple levels, but especially her close connection to Custer for years. Indeed, to Custer, Eliza was much more than another cook and lowly domestic and very much like the cases of Sally Hemings and Essie Mae Washington to their respective politicians of the South: the primary thesis of this current book, which breaks new ground by going where generations of historians have previously refused to trod because of the controversial nature of this long-ignored subject, the Custer--Eliza relationship.

Like the seemingly endless number of American historians and writers who had long shied away from this subject, this current author is fully aware of the controversial nature of this ultra-sensitive subject, because of the fact that Americans have long placed Custer on the Mount Olympus of national heroes, including to this day.

In consequence, this current book was written with the overall objective not to diminish the image or character of Custer, but only to illuminate the complexities of his personality and to reveal the real person by exploring the most forgotten aspect of his life, which historians have long ignored and effectively silenced: the intimate relationship between him and Eliza Denison Brown.

As noted, the primary objective of his current author is not to malign Custer's character. After all, this current author has written several other books about Custer and they have presented an extremely positive image of America's most famous cavalier, especially the 2017 book *Death at the Little Bighorn* and the 2019 book *Custer at Gettysburg*. Both books, which were featured by the History Book Club, have presented new views and perspectives about both the Battle of Little Bighorn and the Battle of Gettysburg, while presenting Custer in a very favorable light by bestowing full credit where it was due.

In many ways, it was somewhat symbolic that Custer achieved his most important and strategic battlefield success at Gettysburg, Pennsylvania, and Eliza came into his life not long thereafter, while he was campaigning with his cavalrymen and Elizabeth was yet back at her home in Monroe, Michigan. At this time in the summer of 1863, Custer was basking in the glory that he and his hard-fighting Michigan cavalrymen had recently won on the East Cavalry Field on the battle's final day of decision, July 3.

Not long after having been promoted to brigadier general in late June 1863 and becoming a dynamic leader of the high-spirited troopers of the Michigan Cavalry Brigade, Custer played the leading role in stopping the serious threat of "Jeb" Stuart's cavalry from striking from the west and into the rear of the over-extended and thin defensive lines of General George Gordon Meade's Army of the Potomac on

Cemetery Ridge at the time of Pickett's Charge. Meanwhile, Custer fought in the army's rear several miles to the east of where "Pickett's Charge" struck its hard-hitting blow, rising to the challenge to save the day.

During the fierce combat that raged between the respective armies on the East Cavalry Field, Custer personally led two headlong charges of his Michigan troopers to the stirring battle-cry of "Come On, You Wolverines!" Custer's aggressiveness and daredevil leadership style sapped the strength of Stuart's cavalry, including experienced horse artillery that could have blasted holes in Meade's rear from the east. Although often not bestowed with sufficient credit in the historical record and as noted, Custer and his men saved the day to ensure that Confederate cavalry never struck from the east into the rear of Meade's defenders along Cemetery Ridge at the most crucial moment during the climactic showdown on Cemetery Ridge.

Eliza's life changed forever when Custer and his bluecoat troopers entered the Northern Virginia Piedmont of Rappahannock County near where she worked as a household slave on a planation. Taking the chance when the Yankees cavalry, which was keeping an eye on the movements of Lee's cavalry not long after the Battle of

Gettysburg that ended on July 3 after the failure of Pickett's Charge, was nearby, Eliza made her move. She boldly struck out on her own from the only life that she had ever known. Displaying her usual resourcefulness, Eliza escaped her master and left slavery behind forever in Rappahannock County and literally never looked back.

In the hope of beginning a new life as a free woman for the first time in her life, she fled to the nearest troops in blue—elements of Custer's cavalry, Army of the Potomac. It is not known if Eliza escaped on her own or if she slipped away with a small group of slaves from the same owner and from the same plantation. All the while, Eliza dodged Confederate cavalry patrols, scouts, and white civilians, who would have gained a nice financial reward from the owner for her capture.

Here, in the encampment of white tents at Amissville, Virginia, in Rappahannock County, Eliza entered the comforting refuge of Custer's cavalry encampment of Meade's Army of the Potomac during August of 1863, after Lee's last invasion of the North had been repulsed at the conclusion of the three days of bloodletting at Gettysburg. Wearing her trademark bandana and a calico dress, Eliza sighed a sense of great relief upon reaching this safe haven of Custer's Yankees at a time when a blue uniform equated to blissful freedom.

With a new lease on life, she joined a sizeable number of other Virginia slaves who had escaped their masters and found refuge among the Yankees, whose war was a holy one to liberate the slaves, after President Abraham Lincoln had issued his Emancipation Proclamation on January 1, 1863—an earth-shaking development that Eliza and other slaves in the Rappahannock County area were already fully aware, because of the active slave grapevine.

Having recently been bestowed with a brigadier general's rank only days before the bloody showdown at Gettysburg, Custer first saw Eliza among the large group of black refugees who had just escaped Virginia slavery. The general was taken not only by Eliza's striking appearance of a shapely and erect carriage, but also by her feisty attitude and spirted nature. Only in her mid-twenties, Eliza was attractive, solidly-built, and healthy, while distinguished by a coal-black complexion of her African ancestors.

Wearing the plainest of apparel that was common to slaves, she was not beautiful in a classic sense to almost all whites because of her pronounced African features and very dark color, which revealed that she was pure African. However, Eliza still possessed a pristine and untainted natural beauty that would have been far more appreciated, if she had been in the land of her ancestors—most likely West Africa--, from where either her parents or grandparents had been stolen as part of the lucrative slave trade at some point in the misty past.

Eliza was hardy and resourceful with a distinct air of confidence unlike many other slaves, both male and female, who had been psychologically damaged by years of slavery's oppression, because she was a doer who had long gotten things done for her master in regard to domestic household chores at the main plantation house: well-honed personal qualities which had helped her survive for years and then to have recently escaped the horrors of slavery in the Old Dominion.

Most of all, Eliza was a survivor of a harsh life. She was tough and hardened by life but maintained a spirited nature and sense of humor, which were qualities that Custer appreciated and early ascertained in Eliza. When Custer had first approached her at the Amissville contraband camp, Eliza carefully sized up the handsome young man in a brigadier general's uniform and liked what she saw. Therefore, she answered Custer's offer to join him and his staff with a few simple words: "I reckon I would."

These four words were the beginning of a long-lasting partnership and relationship that were dominated by mutual admiration that was destined to endure for more than half a decade until Elizabeth caused a permanent break between Eliza and the couple in 1869. At that time, Elizabeth (Libbie) unceremoniously dismissed a faithful friend, who had been long considered part of the Custer "family" because of her devotion and good service.

Another forgotten factor played a role in drawing Custer's attention to her while she stood among the other escaped slaves in their contraband camp in late July 1863. Like any young man and only age twenty-three in good health, including in sexual terms, Custer naturally had an eye for pretty and young women and color made no difference to him—white, Indian, or black, especially those women with an exotic look and an overall natural attractiveness.

And to Custer from rural Ohio, hardly any female looked more exotic than Eliza. With traditional West African features and of a coal dark color, she was in her mid-twenties and only a couple years older than Custer, who was age twenty-three at this time.

From what he saw of her at first glance rather than what he had seen Eliza do and as mentioned, Custer had offered Eliza a position to serve him and his fellow officers of his personal staff. At Custer's personal request, she first served as the cook and laundress for him and the officers of his headquarters with a skillful capability that was needed by young men in uniform when far from home.

But in relatively short order, the strong-willed, intelligent, and irrepressible Eliza, who even eventually garnered a rare measure of admiration from her Confederate captors by her spunky defiance and spirited nature when briefly held a prisoner in June 1864, evolved into something much more than an insignificant cook and laundress at Custer's headquarters. In fact, she emerged as an important and influential personality with a voice and spunky attitude with a surprising degree of authority from an early date.

In some ways, this situation was very much of a natural development that was all but inevitable. Eliza possessed her own distinctive way of command, which had been learned from having been given authority over some of the master's other slaves in the main house to manage daily operations. Her old master, an elderly woman, in Rappahannock County had delegated authority to Eliza for the management of all the domestic chores in the so-called "big house," because of her frail condition and advanced age. Consequently, Eliza was early delegated with considerable authority by her master and had proven herself most worthy.

For an extended period, Eliza performed capably in organizing and supervising household of slaves, both males and females, at the main residence. All evidence had indicated that Eliza was not connected with the drudgery of field work like most slaves and that she had long worked in the main house of her owner, like Sally Hemings at Jefferson's Monticello.

In camp and field with the touch of experience, consequently, she served Custer in capably managing his personal and headquarters on a domestic level for most of the war from 1863-1865. While Eliza held down the domestic front at his headquarters, Custer waged war in the field in magnificent fashion in compiling one the most impressive combat records of any cavalry commander during the Civil War.

As noted, Custer's most important contributions were at Gettysburg on the final day of decision, but also included his outstanding success in the Appomattox Campaign when he played a leading role in forcing the Army of Northern Virginia's submission.

However, from beginning to end, Eliza was even more than a behind-the-scenes organizer and supervisor of Custer's domestic affairs at the headquarters of his cavalry brigade. A spunky person of high spirits in her own right and as noted, Eliza had the good fortune of not having been a common field slave on the plantation, which was a development that helped to fuel her confidence and can-do spirit that rose to the fore during the crisis of wartime.

Most of all, she was a hand's on worker who transformed other former slaves into efficient doers at Custer's headquarters by way of her directives, while knowing how to get things accomplished like Custer on the battlefield. In this sense, Custer and Eliza were achievers in their own respective fields of endeavor.

As noted, Eliza had been most fortunate, despite having been trapped in the tight grip of slavery for her entire life. As the former head household of slave workers at the "big house" of her master, she had capably managed the domestic chores of other slaves--the cooking of meals in the formal dining room, cleaning, overall maintenance, etc.

Consequently, Eliza possessed ample personal experience in management skills and coordinating activities of both male and female slaves to get multiple tasks accomplished as desired by her master. In much the same way, she organized domestic support of other ex-slaves who made daily life easier for Custer and his headquarters staff at a large number of separate encampments from 1863 to 1865.

As demonstrated as both a slave and newly-freed woman, Eliza knew how to give orders with the sound of proper and experienced authority, which brought a greater degree of organizational efficiency to the overall domestic functioning of Custer's headquarters encampment of bright, young officers in blue uniforms. While Custer's staff officers were intelligent and highly-capable young men, they lacked experience in organizing domestic chores for themselves. And, most of all and like Custer, they were focused on attempting to win victory in this war.

Filling this gap, Eliza took charge in this specialized department of supervising Custer's headquarters in regard to domestic tasks, just like when she had organized the functioning of her master's household when it came to domestic responsibilities that needed to be accomplished on a daily basis.

Always a good judge of character and attracted to her for a host of personal and professional reasons, Custer had early seen that Eliza possessed a set of unique qualities that could be put to good use at headquarters. New at the job of commanding an entire cavalry brigade of Michigan troopers and as the youngest brigadier general in the Army of the Potomac at only age twenty-three since late June 1863 when he had been promoted to the position of the army's youngest brigadier general, Custer had wisely recognized that he and his staff needed assistance on the domestic front in regard to utilizing the services of a skilled cook and laundress and organizing domestic support of other slaves, and Eliza was well-qualified for the job. In many ways, she was a take charge kind of person and knew how to get things accomplished just like her new boss, Custer.

Even more, Eliza was ambitious and highly motivated, and she made an ideal fit to begin the process of organizing and managing the domestic requirements of the staff of young Union officers, while they were focused on helping to win a war, at the bivouac of Custer's headquarters. Fueling her motivations was the fact that Eliza now worked for her liberators in blue and not her Southern master, while basking in a righteous cause that she considered sacred: her own personal way of fighting for the Union and supporting the war to destroy what she hated the most on his earth, the sinister institution of slavery.

As revealed by Custer's own words and those of Eliza, she evolved into a great deal more to the newly-appointed brigadier general than generally thought or even imagined by generations of historians and scholars, who had either ignored or minimized her key, if not vital, role in Custer's life for an extended period.

From the beginning and most significant, a strong affection and emotional bond were forged and existed between Custer and Eliza. And this deep bond between the two outlasted the Civil War years because they were essentially comrades-in-arms although one was only a civilian, because they were war partners involved during the course of numerous campaigns of the Cavalry Corps, Army of the Potomac.

Although Custer was destined to marry Elizabeth on February 9, 1864 in Monroe, Michigan, when on official leave from his command, it sometimes seemed that Custer was actually closer to Eliza than Elizabeth, because of the many wartime ordeals and challenges that they shared together during one campaign after another, while Custer's wife was safely at home and far from the front during the most challenging times.

Indeed, Custer had a good deal in common with Eliza primarily because he was a common man from rural Ohio with a lowly background, while his wife was the well-educated and socialite daughter of a respected Monroe judge, who basked in his upper-class status and high standing in the community and state. Although he held an elevated rank in a rise that began after having graduated from West Point in the Class of 1861, despite his successes, and to his credit, Custer never lost his common touch.

In the end, high rank and a lengthy string of successes on the battlefield failed to corrupt Custer, who remained very much the young man who had graduated from West Point in 1861 with little expectations or promise—the last in his class. Like Eliza and from the beginning, Custer had to prove himself and demonstrate his abilities in this war, which he accomplished in magnificent fashion year after year.

Custer and Eliza shared the common touch but in different ways that helped to forge a team while campaigning across Virginia and quite unlike the aristocratic Elizabeth. Pampered and spoiled by her dotting father partly because he was a widower, Libbie, as she was called by Custer, had been raised with lofty upper-class expectations by her strict father, who had strongly discouraged her relationship with Custer in the beginning, when his future was not bright.

Much like Custer never lost his common touch, so Elizabeth never lost her aristocratic ways from a blueblood background, which had early attracted the rustic Ohioan like her attractiveness. Indeed, husband and wife were very much opposites, which was not the case with Custer and Eliza.

For a number of reasons, therefore, the development of a close relationship between the two—the Ohio-born general and the former Virginia slave who shared a rural background and the common touch--should not be entirely surprising, especially in a wartime environment and during the stern demands of conflict. For such reasons, only Eliza, who was young like Custer, was destined to faithfully follow one of America's most renowned and popular military men in not one but two wars across a lengthy stretch of America.

The full story of this resilient black female who stood at the center of life at Custer's headquarters year after year during the Civil War and afterward was a remarkable one on multiple levels. To this day, the headquarters life of most Civil War generals has remained a mystery to this day. Therefore, Eliza's story has shed new light on the inner workings of the headquarters experience in the Army of the Potomac and that little-known environment, which has seldom been written about by historians. Eliza was destined to witness some of the stirring moments of American history that were played out in dramatic fashion in two wars by Custer's side, and she would never be the same as a person from these unique experiences.

All in all, Eliza's evolution from a docile slave at an obscure plantation in the Virginia Piedmont to a self-fulfilled person with a surprising degree of authority and managerial skills at Custer's headquarters, Army of the Potomac, was a rather amazing development to say the least. There was no question that Custer was guilty of an unprecedented level of personal indulgence toward her over an extended period that was simply not seen at any other army headquarters between a commander and a former slave, especially one of her gender.

From the beginning, it was clear that Eliza was Custer's special pet, which no doubt protected her from any transgressions—physical and verbal—from any Union soldiers, who often displayed contempt toward ex-slaves, especially women, and ill-treated them. Resulting in some jealousy among others, Eliza was allowed free reign by Custer for the most part at headquarters, where she was in charge like Custer was in charge on the battlefield.

To Custer's credit, he was colorblind when it came to Eliza, which also was a special quality of their relationship, which was rare at a time when no person in society was generally viewed as less deserving of equal and fair treatment than a black female, especially an ex-slave. At this time, some whites even viewed blacks as subhuman and, unfortunately, acted accordingly in their blissful ignorance and racism.

From beginning to end, Eliza proved as loyal to Custer as the hard-riding Michigan troopers of his four cavalry regiments—the 1st, 4th, 5th and 6th Michigan Cavalry Regiments that consisted of hard-fighting men who were known as the Wolverines because of their tenacity and combat prowess--, who he had commanded with outstanding tactical skill to save the day on July 3 at the Battle of Gettysburg.

Custer's command, a full brigade, was one of the best cavalry commands—a truly elite body of fighting men--of the Army of the Potomac. As mentioned, this fact was most forcefully demonstrated when the Michigan troopers rose splendidly to the challenge of facing Lee's finest cavalry at the East Cavalry Field, where Custer had led the way to victory.

From the beginning, Eliza was determined to follow Custer's destiny and rising star wherever it led, either in the Eastern Theater or on the Great Plains in the years after the Civil War. Year after year, Eliza was often in danger from the threat of Lee's Confederates, especially its hard-hitting cavalry, which included Rebels who would have routinely re-enslaved her if she had been captured, across Virginia. Then, Native American warriors would have either killed or captured Eliza on the Great Plains, if presented the opportunity.

Despite the dangers, she was constantly by Custer's side during some of the most arduous campaigns of the Civil War and during the Indian Wars on the Great Plains and all the way to the end of the momentous decade of the 1860s. Most important and quite unlike any other woman, including Custer's wife, Eliza earned the young general's rare admiration for her savvy, wit, common sense, humor, devotion to duty, perseverance, and other redeeming qualities both as woman and an African American. All in all, this was a measure of respect that Custer rarely bestowed to any other woman.

In total, Eliza served the dashing Midwestern general for six years, from the 1863 to 1869, including for more than half of the Civil War, beginning just after the Battle of Gettysburg, and then on the Great Plains: a solemn, faithful duty to Custer that she continued across half of the North American continent and Eliza never faltered through all the ups and downs. Custer admired Eliza partly because she was as faithful and dependable as a hard-riding Wolverine cavalryman, who he revered as elite fighting men.

First begun by way of mutual consent before Custer married his beloved wife who he wed in early 1864, the relationship between Eliza and Custer, who were both physically attractive individuals in their mid-twenties and early twenties, respectively, in a wartime environment far from home, grew so close that men of the Army of the Potomac, especially in the cavalry corps, spread camp gossip which portrayed them as secret lovers on the tented field during the Civil War years.

Unfortunately, no one knows to this day how the first rumors of sexual intimacy developed between Custer and Eliza. Had a Michigan trooper seen Custer coming from Eliza's tent, which was located near his own in the tented encampment, in the darkness or early morning light before reveille? Had Custer been seen or heard engaged in such intimate activity when a soldier had walked close to Eliza's tent in the middle of the night? This central mystery is simply not known to this day, and no one knows how the rumor first developed.

In fact, Custer's own Michigan soldiers–and not disparaging Union infantrymen or jealous rivals in the officer corps (enemies of Custer from the twin evils of envy and jealousy because of his rapid rise through the ranks and winning ways)--dubbed Eliza "the Queen of Sheba," because of his special preferential treatment of her that was extraordinary at the time.

Eliza's nickname of the "Queen of Sheba" was most appropriate for a number of reasons. According to the Jewish Bible, the Torah, the Queen of Sheba was an ancient black Ethiopian ruler, who had brought gifts and pledges of faithful support to Israel's King Solomon in the ancient past. This analogy was right on target because Eliza received special treatment from Custer and possessed a regal bearing and noble attitude that were in some ways comparable to that of the Queen of Sheba from ancient times.

Most of all, the nickname of the "Queen of Sheba" related to the fact that Custer had pampered her to such an unusual extent and treated Eliza in a special way that was not known to exist between any other Union general and a black female during the Civil War years. To a careful and discreet general with lust on his mind, Eliza would have provided the ideal avenue for a sexual relationship because she was convenient and she would be guaranteed not to tell secrets about Custer that needed to be kept at all costs: certainly some of the key factors that served as an initial inducement for Custer to have made his offer to her, especially before he married.

Of course at this late date by nearly the third decade of the twenty-first century and at long last, the question should be more seriously asked by historians about the truth of the rumors of the intimate nature, including sexual, of this long-forgotten relationship, which was actually much closer than generally acknowledged by top Custer experts and scholars of one of the most closely-analyzed past lives in American history.

By way of comparison, the general acceptance today of the Jefferson--Sally Hemings relationship has been only a relatively recent development that occurred in the late 1990s. This new open-mindedness among the American public about the most famous clandestine interracial relationship in American history resulted when the Jefferson-Hemings relationship was verified by DNA testing.

What cannot be denied was the fact that a very special relationship existed between an attractive and young black female and an attractive and young brigadier general for an extended period of time to a degree unseen elsewhere in the Army of the Potomac: a close bond that had been first forged when both of them were far from home and family during active campaigning in the absence of Elizabeth, who was still at home in Monroe, Michigan.

The giant shadow of the enduring romance of the Custer myth, in which he had been endlessly gloried to this day, has automatically covered-up any hint of the possibility of any kind of a sexual relationship, as alleged at the time by his own men, between Custer and Eliza: the same kind of situation that had long existed in regard to the Sally Hemings—Thomas Jefferson relationship, because of the rise of so many diehard deniers to "protect" the saintly image of the sage of Monticello.

Indeed, the widespread denial of the Jefferson-Hemings relationship was the most common case among the traditional and conservative American historians until the emergence of concrete facts, including DNA testing, in the late 1990s, became known to the public. This development has resulted in today's general acceptance, even by historians, of the fact that a sexual relationship existed between the founding father of the Virginia Piedmont and his young female slave, who was the half-sister of Jefferson's own diseased wife, Martha Skelton, who died in 1782.

Naturally in a predictable development because she was black and because a sexual relationship with an American hero with a lowly former slave were seen by whites as blemishing the romanticized Custer's lofty image and the cherished love story long celebrated between Custer and Elizabeth Clift Bacon-Custer, Eliza has remained a forgotten figure in one of the most written about life stories in which seemingly every aspect of the famous general's life had been explored in great detail.

Quite simply, Eliza and her place in history has been deliberately long silenced because of the giant shadow cast by the Custer mystique, which has overshadowed almost everything and everyone, especially if they were black and nothing more than a former slave.

All in all, this situation has been an unfortunate development, because perhaps nothing has more fully demonstrated the true character of Custer and the real person than his long-overlooked interaction--rather than between him and some of America's most famous politicians and leading personalities of the age--with a person from the lowest rank of society, when they were alone and in private with no one looking to make judgements: an appreciative and thankful black woman who had been just freed from the shackles of slavery and one who Custer treated almost as an equal in the rarest of developments at this time, especially in the Army of the Potomac.

To his credit, Custer was part of a special relationship that was secret, but one that was based on mutual consent and honesty. In today's heated political climate, it has become fashionable among anti-American protestors and radicals to denounce Thomas Jefferson as a child rapist and deface his statues, including even in his native Virginia and at the University of Virginia, Charlottesville, Virginia, which he founded in 1819.

This emotion-laden charge from anti-American extremists and protestors during the summer of 2020 has been based on the premise that Sally Hemings was an unwilling and non-consenting teenage slave when the sexual relationship between her and Jefferson began, although no evidence exists to support this inflammatory charge. While Jefferson's name has been blackened by this ill-founded politically-inspired charge of the most sensational nature, such was never the case in regard to Custer and Eliza because of the factor of mutual consent and since they were near the same age unlike Jefferson and Sally.

By exploring the mysteries of the Custer-Eliza relationship for the first time as much as possible in this current book despite the scant available historical evidence, Custer, the real person, can be gleamed in greater detail and understanding not previously known to generations of Americans.

To his credit in regard to his special relationship with Eliza, Custer has emerged most favorably to contradict the simplistic stereotypical view of Custer as the arrogant egocentric and racist commander, who was consumed with his self-importance at the expense of others, which has long served as a simplistic explanation of the Little Bighorn disaster. However, such was not the case because Custer's record is stainless in his dealings with freed slaves and black women, especially Eliza, in general.

In many ways and as mentioned, the relationship between Custer and Eliza was distinguished by a certain equality and mutual respect rarely seen between a white man and black woman, especially an ex-slave, at this time. Such a situation and a variety of factors have pointed to the existence of not only a special relationship, but also sexual relationship between the two, especially before Custer was married. And in the case of Jefferson and Hemings, this was not an exploitive or abusive kind of intimate relationship between Custer and Eliza, but one based upon mutual attraction and affection, according to all of the available historical evidence.

Most significantly, the long-overlooked story of this former Virginia slave named Eliza Denison Brown has more thoroughly exposed the real human side of the man behind the seemingly endless layers of romanticized Custer myth, because this special relationship thrived for an extended period outside the one widely-celebrated between Custer and Libbie, which became a model of married life virtues to whites during the Victorian Era: the primary factor that has explained why the Custer-Eliza relationship has been silenced for so long by legions of Custer admirers and enthusiasts, who had idolized Custer to no end. The excessive idolization and glorification of their saintly hero guaranteed the silencing of the fundamental truths of the Eliza-Custer story, which has been forgotten.

Most important and as revealed in this current book, this current author's closer and more detailed look at this long-overlooked special relationship that long existed between Eliza and one of America's most respected Civil War heroes has been significant for understanding the real Custer, while revealing more details and basic truths about the life of a lowly former female slave—the most anonymous participants of the Civil War because of their lack of literacy--, who proved to be quite remarkable in a number of ways.

Unfortunately, however, the story of the deep affection that existed between Eliza Brown and Custer for an extended period has been left out of the history book for generations for almost too many reasons to count, because its revelation would have severely tarnished the idolized and glamorized image of a true American hero, who died for his country in the distant Montana Territory: still another example of the silencing of the historical record for personal, political, and professional reasons, while keeping core myths alive and well.

Ironically, the evidence of the most overlooked personal relationship in the entire course of Custer's life has long existed, but the story has not previously been told until the publication of this current book. Custer's own letters–rare revelations to the inner thoughts and soul of the man–have revealed the depth of his affection and admiration for Eliza, who was an amazing woman in her own right, as he fully realized and as revealed in his writings.

Like the words of others who commented about this most secret of relationships that existed in wartime encampments across Virginia in Elizabeth's absence, Custer's words have exposed this long-hidden dimension of his life and the most secret inner soul of one of America's greatest Civil War heroes.

First and foremost, the breaking of new ground in an overcrowded field of study—basically the Civil War (like the subject of Custer) has long been nothing less than a stale historical field primarily because so many volumes have been devoted to America's bloodiest war--and one endlessly romanticized and glorified by countless admiring historians has posed a considerable challenge of the first magnitude to this current writer, especially in regard to Custer.

Essentially an army of traditional and conservative historians have long warmly embraced the enduring romance of the Custer mystique to ensure that the general's most secret relationship has not been exposed to the American people for more than a century and a half.

In the hope of providing a host of new insights into one of the most written about figures in the annals of American military history, the forgotten secret relationship between General Custer and Eliza Brown has been resurrected and brought to life as much as possible in this current book for the first time at this late date.

As mentioned, this close relationship was all but inevitable partly because Custer and Eliza were much alike and about the same age when in close proximity to each other for extended periods to time, while under wartime stresses, including life-of-death situations. Both Eliza and Custer were fun-loving, carefree in spirit and blessed with good senses of humor, which served as one of the central foundations of their close relationship.

In contrast to the common sense and light-hearted Eliza, the often snotty and aristocratic Libbie was a spoiled, pampered, and largely humorless product of the upper-class and daughter of a wealthy judge, who was one of the leading citizens of Monroe. Therefore, Eliza and Elizabeth could not have been more different.

For such reasons, a demanding, selfish Libbie was often a thorn in her husband's side. He, therefore, paid a high price for his love and devotion to her because of his generally easy going nature and light-heartedness for having married up at the first opportunity, when he had impulsively climbed the social ladder without much thought about the personal consequences in regard to the often-overlooked, but inevitable, downside of a long-term relationship with a spoiled member of a higher class than his own.

Quite simply, the relationship between Custer and Eliza was quite the opposite of the traditional relationship that existed between Libbie and Custer in a wide variety of ways that historians have long not dared to explore in detail since its revelations would have been considered heresy, because of the hallowed nature of the Custer marriage, as emphasized by Elizabeth in her prolific writings.

Therefore, despite his intense love for his wife that was genuine after he married the pretty judge's daughter in early 1864 and in general, Custer's overall relationship with Eliza was in many ways more natural, smoother—and certainly less demanding and stressful--, and lighter than with the spoiled Elizabeth. To Custer's delight, the more casual Custer-Eliza relationship was also distinguished by a more playful ease that consisted of teasing and jokes exchanged between the two: much like the fun-filled relationships that he enjoyed with his brothers since boyhood days.

Sex, if that was the case according to camp rumor from Union soldiers and certainly the case because of historical evidence and collaborating accounts, between Custer and Eliza was part of that almost natural equation of a much less complicated and far easier secret relationship, which might well have been fulfilling to Custer in a variety of ways before his marriage and even perhaps afterward, which was much less likely in general, given the available evidence.

After all, Eliza was neither spoiled, ungrateful, or demanding when it came to Custer and quite unlike Elizabeth, posing no stern personal demands or outrageous requests. Therefore, what developed was not only an intimate relationship but also a close friendship between Custer and Eliza that continued for years.

As noted, Custer's inclusive and good-natured personality was more open to the idea of intimate relationships with women of different races because he was entirely open-minded when it came to the female sex. In this regard, Custer certainly did not discriminate and held no prejudices when it came to pretty women. A woman's smile, vibrant personality, and overall personal and sex appeal came in a variety of colors as Custer fully understood and realized. And he acted upon what appealed to him with the same kind of impulsiveness and boldness that he often demonstrated on the battlefield with the headlong cavalry charge.

While a West Pointer who served at the academy from 1857 to 1861, Custer had suffered a bout of venereal disease from having departed the institute on the Hudson, journeyed downriver, and visited New York City, where he dallied with a prostitute. Some historians have speculated that Custer became sterile from this sexual encounter because of a case of venereal disease partly because Elizabeth and Custer never produced any children.

In this context, a relationship with Eliza in the tented encampment of his headquarters was certainly a step-up (an actual relationship based on mutual admiration rather than casual sex) from that seedy and casual form of sex that he had been bought as a sex-starved young cadet. In this sense, the Custer-Eliza union was an interim relationship of a casual nature and one based on mutual consent before he embarked on the most serious relationship of his life with Elizabeth.

Despite a product of the Victorian Age, Custer retained most of his humble eastern Ohio roots from among the rolling hills of Harrison County and rural environment that were almost frontier-like. Therefore, he did not fit the restrictive, conservative mold of upper-class pretensions that existed in the aristocratic Bacon family, including Elizabeth, which hailed from the town of Monroe, Michigan. Quite simply, Custer's wife was an urban product, while Eliza was a rural product like Custer.

By comparison to the upper-class elite of an urban environment, Custer was different. He was a rural midwestern product and almost a frontier type because of his upbringing in rural Ohio at New Rumley as the son of a blacksmith. He was raised among the rolling hills and forests of eastern Ohio and a clear-flowing watercourse that had been named in honor of the town's early settlers, Irish Creek.

Most of all, Custer remained an individualist and thought for himself when it came to his personal life, especially before his marriage: another secret of his outstanding successes on the battlefield partly because he was tactically flexible and not bound like an obedient slave by what he had learned at West Point, where he had been the goat of his class and learned far less than his classmates or so it seemed.

In this sense and in personal terms and especially while in private, Custer was not bound by convention or custom in the frontier tradition. Even while wearing a general's uniform and when in private beyond the eyes of his men while campaigning in the field, he remained a free spirit not bound by strict societal dictates and this Custer spirit and open-mindedness formed the core of his unorthodox personality: a situation and predisposition that helped to set the stage for his intimate secret relationship with a former slave of the opposite sex.

Indeed, such a clandestine personal relationship was in keeping with Custer's unconventional style, and fun-loving and free-wheeling ways, especially before he married Elizabeth. Quite simply, Custer was as free-thinking and unorthodox on the battlefield as he was in bedroom, before he was married and settled down, because of his intense love for his wife.

Custer was certainly neither a sexual prude or stereotypical Victorian who only engaged in sex with his wife, a sexually repressed male, or the legendary golden boy without a host of personal vices, including lust and sexual escapades, that have long been either minimized or long-overlooked entirely by generations of historians, who have placed Custer on the Mount Olympus of American heroes.

However, in truth, Custer committed no great moral infraction by engaging in love-making with Eliza before he was married, because it was a mutual consent relationship that hurt no one. Instead and although it cannot be proven and is not known, such an intimate relationship at this time might have even added to Custer's mental balance and well-being under the immense stresses of war that only fueled his ultra-energetic performances on the battlefield in his bids to destroy the enemies of his country.

Admiring Custer historians, who seemingly never cease extolling the virtues of the Civil War's golden boy, have conveniently ignored the general's extracurricular sexual activities to fit neatly the much-touted romance of the Custer legend and the glorified myth, especially the idealized one created by Libbie in her prolific writings, after her beloved husband's death at the Little Bighorn on a tragic afternoon that changed her life forever: a situation which required a chivalric knight in a blue uniform and celibate romantic war hero before his marriage and then a perfect husband of almost-saintly character, who conformed to Victorian Age values of a proper ideal officer and a gentleman in the most stereotypical fashion. Of course, the romanticization of the perfect Custer marriage of an ideal couple was only part of the Custer myth that was utterly divorced from reality.

As confirmed by contemporaries, including soldiers who served during both the Civil War and Indian Wars, no truth existed in regard to the much-heralded validity to the romanticized myth of the Victorian Era that Custer only made love to one woman in his entire life, including during the Civil War years, as alleged in Libbie's own prolific writings that have glorified her husband to no end: all of which has led us to believe the stainless image of Custer that Elizabeth desired for immortality.

To maintain the heroic Custer image that had been endlessly romanticized by countless authors and as mentioned, the long-ignored aspect of secret sexual activity in this vigorous, healthy, and handsome young man's life has been noticeably absent in almost all of the many Custer biographies, despite emphasis of his youthful energy and vigor as a cavalry commander on the battlefield. However, battlefield and bedroom energy were in fact closely linked and part of Custer's personality: a forgotten secret of his successes.

Maintaining the enduring romance of the outsized Custer legend has long required the presentation of an untarnished mythical hero rather than the ordinary and common man with the same vices, weaknesses, and biological needs like any man, especially when it came to sex.

Any possibility or the mere thought that the allegedly-saintly Custer might have been a womanizer or engaged in sex either before or during—or both--his marriage and behind Libbie's back, has been practically unthinkable, because of the power of the Custer mythology. Worst of all to the legions of faithful Custer worshipers who are mostly traditional white males, the possibility of Custer having sex with a black woman has been almost beyond the comprehension of the Custer cult followers, who still mindlessly cling to their white idol with a religious-like reverence: allegedly, the same perceived ultimate horror of horrors once widely held among so many Jefferson admirers, before the Sally Hemings relationship became not only much better known, but also has been accepted by the American public with the discovery of DNA evidence in the late 1990s.

Therefore, despite the evidence, Custer's secret sex life with this remarkable Virginia woman of African descent has been overlooked and ignored by generations of white historians: just like Jefferson historians in regard to Sally Hemings until only recently. Most significant and as noted, this secret relationship between Custer and Eliza was certainly not ignored by Civil War soldiers and the troopers who served in the ranks of the 7th Cavalry at the time, however.

After all and in general, white Custer admirers have been long far more intent on preserving the romantic Custer myth and glorified legend than accepting the historical facts, including the exact details about the final showdown at the Little Bighorn, while dominated by a subconscious and almost subliminal racism: factors that have ensured that Eliza had been long nonexistent as a person in their white-only and dominant cultural views in regard to the writing of Custer's story.

Following in Elizabeth's footsteps as revealed in her prolific writings in three books and articles that promoted Custer's memory and reputation against all critics during the more than half century that she lived after his husband's death, generations of Custer admirers in their writings have emphasized the strength of the much-touted stainless romance between Custer and Libbie to highlight his sterling virtues as a man, husband, Christian, and modern knight in a blue uniform. In most of the seemingly endless number of books about Custer, almost all warts or blemishes have been eliminated to present the most pristine image of a man who bravely died for his country.

To maintain the lofty perch of the excessively-romanticized Custer image that has reached mythological proportions like few other military men in the annals of American military history, the mere possibility that Custer might have engaged in a sexual relationship, even if consensual and especially if loving, as alleged with Eliza was considered dirty and shameful from the traditional white point-of-view. Consequently, the rumors of this special relationship had to be swept under the rug and forgotten by historians in a repeat of what had initially happened to the ample body of historical evidence about the longtime Jefferson-Hemings relationship in the hilltop privacy of Monticello.

Therefore, Custer biographers, almost all male, white, and conservative, have long either minimized or ignored the depth of the relationship that existed between Custer and Eliza partly because of the dominance of their own racial belief systems and traditional cultural views that white women, even an ugly one, as far more preferable, especially in regard to beauty, to black women, even the most beautiful ones, on every possible level, because of lifelong cultural indoctrination and racial prejudices.

Like the generations of white Sally Heming—Thomas Jefferson relationship deniers, they have strongly felt the need to silence this long-overlooked story about a secret relationship enjoyed by their saintly hero, almost as if fearing that if this chapter of Custer's life was explored in greater detail, then something most disturbing might be discovered under the thick layers or romance and myth: the unvarnished truth stemming from the verification of an extremely close relationship, and a degree of actual human affection that had been demonstrated between a revered white war hero and a black woman of lowly background.

Of course, this realization would have been the worst imaginable scenario for generations of Custerphiles, who have long enthusiastically embraced the Custer gospel, while faithfully worshipping at the altar of Custer mythology and romance.

In overall terms, this situation has been an almost inevitable development that has resulted in a historical silencing has been most unfortunate, ensuring that key aspects of the Custer story have been deemed entirely insignificant and then reduced to little more than obscure footnotes, because they failed to support the romantic Custer myths.

However, to fully understand Custer, this most forgotten aspect of his secret life—the long-ignored story of Eliza and the depth of her affection for Custer--will be now explored in this current book in greater detail than ever before by cutting through the seemingly endless layers of glorification and romantic myths (a true Gordian Knot) that has long covered-up the real Custer like a holy shroud: the motivation for the writing of this current book to present the most forgotten chapter of the Custer story.

Therefore, unlike the seemingly endless number of books that have long focused on the traditional view of Custer as the much celebrated and overly-romanticized war hero, who chased glory and tempted fate too many times until even his legendary "Custer's luck" finally ran out along the Little Big Horn on June 25, 1876, this current "new look" book has shed new light on the real Custer, the man and human being and not the usual romantic symbol and embellished legend: ironically, in his own time, Custer was an anachronism of a bygone age that was never as romantic or glorious, like the Indian Wars and life on the western frontier in general, as long portrayed by later-day armchair historians for generations.

Significantly, long hidden from view by the multiple layers of Custer legend of romance and myth, the most ignored but yet most revealing story of the close personal relationship between Custer and Eliza Brown has been nothing less than the greatest and most silenced secret of the Custer legend.

Even though this rather astonishing fact will not be accepted or even fully understood by Custerphiles even at this late date, the special relationship that existed for years between George Armstrong Custer and Eliza Brown has been exposed for the first time in this current book: the most forgotten and ignored chapter of the Custer saga.

As mentioned, this current book was not written to diminish the enduring image or legacy of Custer, or what he accomplished in faithfully serving his country with distinction and great courage over an extended period of time. The primary purpose of this current book has been to present the most forgotten chapter of the Custer story for the first time to reveal as much as possible about the real man at this late date.

Interestingly and as noted, Thomas Jefferson had also felt deep affection and had a sexual relationship with another black woman from Virginia decades before Custer. Less than a decade and a half after Jefferson's July 4, 1826 death on the republic's birthday, Custer had been born in New Rumley, eastern Ohio, on December 5, 1839.

Union soldiers, including Custer, viewed Monticello with reverence, after Custer, who was leading Phil Sheridan's cavalry, had accepted the surrender of Charlottesville on March 3, 1865, before the Appomattox Campaign. It is not known if Custer knew anything about Sally Hemings at the time. Eliza, who was still with Custer's command during this early 1865 campaign, certainly did not know about this mixed-race African American female, who played such a meaningful role during a lengthy period of Jefferson's life.

For the first time and despite the seemingly endless number of books that have focused on the amazing life of George Armstrong Custer, this current book has explored the unique theme of race and sex in Custer's life that has been long ignored by generations of historians in a belated view, which has been long-needed a fresh and new perspective to illuminate an old, overly-embellished story. The close personal relationship that long existed between Custer and Eliza on an intimate level was certainly Custer's greatest secret, which died with him at the Little Bighorn in the end, and one that has escaped generations of historians until now with the publication of this current book.

Even more than the story of the long-overlooked personal relationship between Custer and Eliza, this current book has revealed the life of a remarkable African American women long regulated to the obscurity and the shadowy background of the Custer story like so many African

Americans, especially women, throughout the course of American history.

In the prolific writings about Custer for more than a century and a half, Eliza has served as little more than a background prop that has been completely overshadowed by the highly-romanticized relationship between Custer and his wife, which was celebrated for decades during the Victorian Era. Therefore, this current book has focused on the life of a former slave woman more than the life of Custer to reveal a forgotten chapter of the African American experience.

What has been revealed in this current book is the life of a young and irrepressible Virginia woman of African heritage who demonstrated an amazing degree of courage, perseverance, and compassion that often out-shined those more famous personalities who surrounded her. Most important, these sterling qualities ensured that Eliza would not only survive but also ultimately thrive in a too-often cruel world that had stacked all the odds against her only because of her sex and color.

Most important, Custer greatly admired Eliza as a person because she possessed the kind of personal qualities that he had long esteemed in any person. For understandable reasons and especially since she had survived the horrific ordeal of slavery, Custer was amazed by this young black woman's strength of character partly because some of Eliza's best qualities were lacking in his own wife, because of her pampered and aristocratic background as the rich judge's daughter.

Therefore, revealing that Eliza was an unique, if not dynamic, person in her own right and who was on his mind and much more than admitted by generations of admiring historians, General Custer often wrote freely in his letters to his wife about this former slave, who had come into his life quite by accident, while campaigning in Rappahannock County, Northern Virginia: a young woman who he had an inordinate amount of admiration and respect for from beginning to end.

Thanks to the high profile of Custer and his wife who became America's most idealized husband and wife team after the Civil War and during the Victorian period partly because of their prolific writings in the popular press, the real person known as Eliza Brown has finally emerged in this current book as a remarkable individual in own right and an unique person of substance in not only one, but two of America's wars.

In regard to the writing of this current book, the overall goal of this current author has been to bring a new level understanding to one of the most popular military leaders in the annals of American military history, while revealing the life of a remarkable former slave named Eliza as much as possible. This current book—the first ever devoted to the forgotten Custer-Eliza relationship--has fully demonstrated that the old argument (another myth) that there is nothing new or important that can be added to the much-written story of Custer's life is entirely wrong.

Phillip Thomas Tucker, Ph.D.

Central Florida

September 3, 2020

Part I

Chapter I

Escape from Slavery

The life of a slave woman named Eliza Denison Brown was changed forever when she decided to take the great risk of attempting to escape her lifelong bonds of slavery during the summer of 1863. Clearly, to this young woman from the rolling hills of the Virginia Piedmont, the sweet taste of freedom was well worth the considerable risk of making the desperate gamble to escape slavery's horrors that she had known all her life.

Eliza had lived her dreary life as a lowly slave not far from the small village, which was the largest that was situated near her owner's plantation, Amissville. This quaint agricultural community was located in the eastern part of Rappahannock County amid the bountiful and fertile lands of Northern Virginia.

Here, in the Virginia Piedmont in the picturesque foothills of the Blue Ridge Mountains situated around sixty miles west of the nation's capital of Washington, D.C., Eliza had been a slave for her entire life, evidently on the same Rappahannock County plantation where she worked without compensation in early 1863. She had been raised in a prosperous state known as the Old Dominion, which had witnessed the insidious birth of slavery in America at the port of Jamestown, Virginia, in 1619.Jamestown was at the first permanent English settlement in North America, and what happened there set the stage for the coming of a massive number of enslaved Africans in the future.[1]

Here, in the Piedmont of the Old Dominion which slave-owner Thomas Jefferson had called his home around the town of Charlottesville, Virginia, that was located around 60 miles to the southwest of Amissville and despite its horrors, the institution of slavery was more benign, especially in Eliza's Rappahannock County, than in the Deep South. However, the degree of the institution's less severity was only in relative terms compared to the sprawling cotton plantations of the Deep South.

Fortunately, for Eliza in her lifetime of servitude, this more favorable reality existed because Virginia engaged in more diversified agriculture beyond the one-crop staple of cotton cultivation like in the Deep South, including the raising of corn and wheat. Virginia had long been the mother of the slave states in power and prestige, containing the largest black slave population for most of America's existence and during the Civil War period.

Here at Jamestown and as noted, the first slaves had set foot on American soil when a "Dutch" ship unloaded a small group of slaves at the English colony in 1619 around 150 miles southeast of Amissville. The port of Jamestown was situated on the shore of the James River that led to the broad waters of tidal Chesapeake Bay and then on to the vast expanse of the turbulent Atlantic. In a historical development, what was set ashore in late August 1619 at the Jamestown Colony was nothing less the vital human resource that ensured the economic boom of Virginia for future generations.

Thanks to the cash crop of tobacco that had served as the early economic foundation of the colony, slavery thrived in Virginia, especially in the tidewater. Tobacco had been the state's most lucrative crop during the seventeenth and eighteenth centuries, transforming the Old Dominion into a rich tobacco kingdom second to none.

The booming tobacco kingdom made Virginia immensely profitable from the beginning of settlement, before spreading west over the Appalachian Mountains to the border states of Kentucky during the eighteenth century and then into

Missouri during the nineteenth century on the west side of the Mississippi River, which was part of the historic push of the American people toward the setting sun.

But more important, the rise of slavery coincided with the rise of freedom on American soil, from the beginning of settlement, including in New England, and especially in Virginia, for average white settlers. This paradoxical development helped to pave the way to greater freedom that partly led to the outbreak of the American Revolution, the Declaration of Independence, and the creation of a new nation conceived in liberty, even though the new republic was the world's largest slave-owning republic: one of the great ironies of American history that has continued to haunt the American nation to this day.[2]

For the American nation, the institution of slavery and Eliza Denison Brown in the Virginia Piedmont, history had finally come full circle in the Old Dominion by the summer of 1863, after the nightmare of the Civil War had erupted in full force in the spring of 1861: America's greatest national nightmare that began when Confederate cannon opened fire on Fort Sumter in the harbor of Charleston, South Carolina, on an April day that Americans never forgot.

In its most basic form, this vicious conflict, or the oddly called brother's war in a nickname that almost seemed to mock the insanity of war because this was the bloodiest conflict in the nation's history, was all about America's central contradiction and dilemma, slavery.

Of course, slavery was America's darkest curse and this brutal war was the divided nation's "time on the cross" in what was a cruel repayment for long-existing national sins not only in the South, but also in the North. After all, slavery had existed in every state at the time of the American Revolution, and the northeast, including Puritan New England, had economically profited immensely from the lucrative slave trade at an early date.

Indeed, as earlier in England, enterprising merchants, industrialists, and bankers in the northeastern United States had long profited from the booming slave trade to fuel the rise of the industrial revolution on both sides of the Atlantic. Even the early economy of New England had been closely tied to slavery and the booming slave trade, especially after the pious New Englanders, including colony founders, decided that Africans were far more reliable and cost effective permanent labor source than Native Americans, who they had enslaved.

Captured in wartime, Native Americans of various tribes in New England had either died off or had been long sold into slavery on the British sugar islands of the West Indies, extinguishing entire tribes like the ill-fated Pequot. Africans then filled the void left by the enslaved Native Americans for the task of developing a new land.

From the beginning in what had been a true Faustian Bargain, consequently, North and South had been bound by an unholy alliance in fueling and profiting from slavery for the transformation of a rugged land that needed to be tamed at all costs. And it had taken both black and white to tame it, transforming the frontier into a developed land of plenty. In the making of America and as noted, slavery had early served the central foundation of the robust economies of the more industrialized North and the more rural South for generations before the Civil War.

By the time that Eliza planned to flee the hated institution of slavery and her narrowly-focused world of a small corner of Rappahannock County in Virginia, where the capital of the Confederacy was located on the muddy James River (like Jamestown) around one hundred miles to the southeast at Richmond, Virginia.

Unknown to her at the time, the struggle to determine the Confederacy's fate was destined to be decided on the strategic ground of Virginia. General Robert E. Lee's Army of Northern Virginia had been early assigned to defend Virginia, that most striking paradoxical development that had early became permanently entrenched–the simultaneous rise of slavery and freedom in America that had led to the dominance of the "peculiar institution" across the South–, and an independent Southern republic based upon slavery.

Therefore, the South's overly-ambitious experiment in nationhood that had been initiated with heady enthusiasm in February 1861 existed on the concept of liberty resting on the flimsy foundation of human servitude, while a more enlightened western Europe, especially England, had already turned its back on its own system of slavery earlier in the nineteenth century.[3]

Without hopes or expectations for a bright future, Eliza had been born around 1840 in Rappahannock County and raised on a plantation located about a mile east of the Ben Venue. The Ben Venue was a 1,500-acre plantation and a rural crossroads situated on commanding high ground of a timbered ridge, which overlooked the Blue Ridge to the west.

Here, about four miles northwest of Amissville, Virginia, and southeast of Front Royal nestled in the Shenandoah Valley situated on the mountain's other side, and unlike the typical small log structure occupied by Eliza in the slave quarters, the slaves of William V. Fletcher, who owned Ben Venue, lived in three brick houses with chimneys: slave quarters generally unseen for slaves in cotton country of the Deep South.

Fletcher's two-story stone mansion stood across from the small cabins of the single-room slave quarters, which consisted of brick structures of a style (stone) comparable to the sprawling mansion for the owner's vanity more than his slave's welfare. As typically the case in a symbolic layout by deliberate design, the Ben Venue mansion stood before the slave quarters in commanding fashion, dominating it on higher ground.

It is not known how many of Eliza's family members likewise lived on the plantation with her besides her mother. However, it was likely that both of her parents and other siblings were still living or had once lived at this remote place in the Piedmont that she had long called home.

Eliza's father might have been a free man who had moved to the free state of Pennsylvania located just to the north or he might have been a slave who had suffered the cruel fate of having been sold "downriver." Even where slavery dominated every aspect of life, this remote place in Rappahannock County was home to Eliza.

Here, the Virginia Piedmont region situated just east of the Blue Ridge Mountains, where the fertile Shenandoah Valley lay just to the west on the mountain's other side, and amid the foothills of the picturesque Blue Ridge that dominated the horizon to the west, stood in the eye of the conflict's storm.

With confidence and flags flying near the beginning of the Gettysburg Campaign, the troops of General Lee's Army had passed through such remote, but vital, rural crossroads like Ben Venue to reach the all-important gaps in the Blue Mountains, which allowed them to gain the Shenandoah Valley to continue the march north. The South's primary eastern army eventually met with a rendezvous with destiny and a decisive defeat at the market community, strategic crossroads, and college town of Gettysburg, Adams County, Pennsylvania.

Therefore, as fate would have it, Eliza and the plantation upon which she lived literally stood at the center of the movements of the two principal opposing Civil War armies, the Army of the Potomac and the Army of Northern Virginia. And this region's importance only continued after Lee's defeat at Gettysburg, when the mauled Army of Northern Virginia retired south.

Because of the strategic position of Rappahannock County and because Lee's battered army had to pass south through this region of plenty that provided ample provisions, Eliza Brown was about gain the opportunity of joining one of the Union's cavalry commands shadowing Lee's retreat south and passing through her own homeland. And as noted, this cavalry unit of young men and boys in blue uniforms just happened to be under the command of a young Ohio-born officer of promise, George Armstrong Custer. He had been promoted to brigadier general just before the three-day slaughter at Gettysburg, where he had excelled on the bloody afternoon of July 3.[4]

Amid the wooded foothills of the Blue Ridge Mountains that looked blue from a distance to have early garnered their name from the early settlers who had been mostly Scotch-Irish, Eliza had served as a house servant on a plantation in eastern Rappahannock (an Algonquian word) County, which contained 3,120 slaves in 1860.

Despite trapped in the tight grip of slavery, she was one of the lucky ones. Although blessed with good health and a stout build that was ideal for working in the fields, Eliza was not a common field hand by the time of the Civil War, because she possessed culinary skills and a knack for organizing and directing other slaves in domestic labor at the main household.

In consequence, Eliza enjoyed a close relationship with her owner, an older Virginia woman, demonstrating an uncanny ability to get along with whites. Most of all, Eliza also proved that she was able to get the job done, when she had been assigned to undertaking specific tasks. Therefore, organizing and supervising the domestic help at the main house became Eliza's primary duty at the "big house."

In fact, Eliza even possessed a degree of affection for this older white woman, and she called her "ole Missus," who treated her well. After the war ended and despite a free woman for two years, Eliza still felt a good deal of concern for this older woman's welfare in war-ravished Virginia.

Eliza's well-placed concerns resulted in a postwar visit to her old plantation on her own, thanks to Custer's permission for her to undertake the journey. Of course, the fact of her benevolent obsessiveness about her former owner's welfare indicated that Eliza had been relatively well-treated in the past and had a big heart.

Clearly, Eliza possessed a distinct open-mindedness and surprising little animosity toward whites, including former slave-owners and despite slavery's horrors: one personal quality that later explained why she was a special person, which was a positive factor in her relationship with Custer.

The little existing evidence has indicated that this older Virginia woman of Rappahannock County and Eliza's owner was a widow, which guaranteed her heavier reliance on Eliza by the time of the Civil War. A large amount of trust had been established between Eliza and her white owner and a permanent bond existed between them that held firm even after the Civil War ended.

Therefore, Eliza was more familiar with whites than the typical field slave on the plantation, working closely with them in the "big house" and interacting with the master's family, and her kind "old Missus," in Eliza's own words. All the while, she demonstrated abundant skills in domestic and servant tasks, including organizational.[5]

For such reasons, Eliza early gained confidence in herself and her abilities, including because of her good relationship with her owner and in organizing support among the slaves for performing duties at the main residence on the Rappahannock County plantation. Clearly, Eliza was a favored slave and benefitted from relatively decent treatment, especially when compared to field slaves.

Unfortunately, because of the lack of documentation and she wrote (Eliza was an illiterate slave) nothing about her life, very little is known about Eliza's family. But she was not entirely on her own because her mother was still alive, after the deaths or sales of other close relatives by the time of the Civil War. This fact partly explained how Eliza learned to fend for herself, developing a degree of resourcefulness and can-do attitude that served her well both inside and outside of slavery.

Unfortunately, nothing has been discovered about Eliza's father, except that he was an African who perhaps had been born in the distant motherland and almost certainly had been a slave in this remote area of Rappahannock County. Therefore, he perhaps lived on the same plantation as Eliza, although it cannot be known with any degree of certainty. However, if still living and if her father was yet a slave in Virginia, then he might have been living in an adjoining county of the Virginia Piedmont, or father south in central or southern Virginia.

If Eliza's mother, who was still alive during the Civil War as noted, had been a house servant like her daughter, then she would have been taught some domestic skills to her daughter from her own past experiences in having dealt closely with her masters, while passing down a legacy that served the young woman well for the rest of her life.[6]

Indeed, despite her relative youth by 1863 when in her mid-twenties, Eliza possessed the ability to operate not only an entire house of black domestic slaves, but also certain aspects of the plantation, even in the absence of whites. As mentioned, Eliza's master was a widow who had needed assistance and the capable Eliza was just the kind of person to fill the void, after the death of the widow's husband.

Therefore, by the time of the Civil War, Eliza basked in a high level of confidence and trust, which displayed her maturity, ample capabilities, and good old fashioned common sense that she put to ample use on a daily basis, while working in the "big house." This situation has also indicated that the "old Missus" was elderly, which bestowed upon Eliza an extra amount of duties and responsibilities in excess of those normally given by a master to a young female slave. However, Eliza had early demonstrated that she was up to the challenge of increased responsibilities.[7]

Clearly, Eliza benefitted from her mother's teaching and wisdom which helped to make her wise, or "sage," beyond her years as revealed in Custer's words from a June 28, 1864 letter. In personal terms, she had also benefitted from the close-knit and supportive slave community that acted as a surrogate family, while providing a kinship system in the depths of servitude that allowed for a greater degree of personal growth and development.

In relative terms, the institution of slavery in the Old Dominion and in the United States in general allowed for the all-important development of the monogamous slave family unlike on the sugar islands in the Caribbean, such as Cuba

(Spanish) and Jamaica (English), where imbalances between the numbers of male and female slaves were far greater than in America to hamper traditional family development.[8].

In consequence, a more vibrant slave community developed on American soil in which the average slave embraced a distinctive African-based culture, especially from sundown to sunup, from the distant motherland and one that was distinguished by languages, ancient customs, and belief systems entirely different from those European-based ones of the white masters.

Likewise surviving in the slave community, which had a self-fulfilling life of its own, were distinctive aspects of African religion, spiritualism, musical traditions, dancing and singing, and a rich social life: all factors that benefitted the lives of the average slave, including Eliza.

These key factors, including the cherished ways of ancestor worship and retaining aspects of African culture and folkways, served as a buffer for young slaves to the most devastating effects of slavery, while bolstering a sense of confidence and self-esteem to black women like Eliza: a tough and harsh forge of severe adversity that resulted in hard-earned experiences which strengthened the individual, including female slaves.[9]

However almost like a miracle from God's hand, everything had suddenly changed for Eliza and many other Virginia slaves because of the dismal failure of America's political system and politicians, when polarization between North and South became complete and the war erupted to change their lives forever. As never before, freedom was in the air for enslaved African Americans and Africans after the nation had been plunged into the nightmare of the Civil War, when the arrival of Union troops brought liberation to Virginia's slaves.

During the first two years of the conflict while young men and boys across America slaughtered each other for what they believed was right, especially in Virginia which became the scene of the bloodiest battles, Eliza remained on the plantation in Rappahannock County with her mother. All the while, both sides' primary opposing armies (the Army of Northern Virginia and the Army of the Potomac) battled on Virginia soil in desperate attempts to gain possession of the other's capital, Washington, D.C. and Richmond, Virginia. As fate would have it, the two capitals were separated by only around 150 miles of the war-torn Old Dominion.

At the time of her escape from slavery during the summer of 1863 and like other slaves in Rappahannock County, Virginia, Eliza had already heard by way of the slave grapevine about President Abraham Lincoln's final Emancipation Proclamation that had been issued from the White House on January 1, 1863.

In addition, she almost certainly heard about acts of sabotage and outright resistance to slavery by other slaves from her home county and the surrounding area, because they knew that this war was about slavery and white folks were dying in large numbers in consequence: an entirely unprecedented situation that led to the most eventful occurrences and experiences in Eliza's lifetime.

Resistance to the nightmare of slavery began before the firing on Fort Sumter on April 12, 1861. One former slave from Rappahannock County, Virginia, Dangerfield Newly, had been a member of John Brown's raiders. They had captured the United States Arsenal at Harper's Ferry, Virginia, in October 1859 in the desperate hope of sparking slave revolts across the nation to forever destroy the hated institution.

An Ohioan like Custer, the Holy Bible-influenced Brown was a true holy warrior. He commanded a revolutionary force of blacks and whites: a truly integrated miniature army of righteous liberators, who were united in their mutual hatred of slavery.

The son of a Scottish father and slave mother, Newby had been born a slave in Virginia's Shenandoah Valley in 1815 during the War of 1812. He was eventually freed by his loving father, whose vivid memories of his ancient Scottish homeland across the sea were still vivid.

However, Newby's life became enormously complicated because his beloved wife and seven children were still mired in slavery's dark depths. They were owned by an unsympathetic Jesse Jennings, who presented Newby with zero discount price for gaining his family's freedom by purchase. In consequence, the thoroughly-vexed Newby needed the enormous sum of $1,500 to free his family. Out of sheer desperation to free his family, Newby cast his fate with John Brown and his desperate bid to destroy slavery.

To free his long-suffering family, Newby fought beside Brown during one of the most desperate raids in American history. However, Brown's raid on Harpers Ferry ended in disaster. The Bible-quoting Brown was fated to be hung on December 2, 1859 after his capture at Harpers Ferry and the resulting disaster. Brown's great hope of inciting the slave revolts across the South had failed miserably.

However, the inspirational legacy of these black revolutionaries, like Newby who was killed during the raid, who fought in the ranks led by the slavery-hating John

Brown never died. These brave men became martyrs, like their beloved leader, and they were not soon forgotten by the young men, both black and white, of the North.

During this war to save the Union and partly inspired by John Brown and his black and white raiders who had died in their ill-fated bid to forever end of the curse of slavery, black soldiers, who mostly had been slaves, of the United States Colored Troops (USCT), were destined to serve with distinction from 1863-1865.

These highly-motivated black fighting men in blue uniforms included former slaves from Rappahannock County. During the Civil War years, they served with pride that was shared by Eliza and other slaves because this was a righteous war of liberation. No doubt Eliza knew some of these black men in blue uniforms from her home area before the war.

Eventually, more than 200,000 USCT troops served the Union, providing invaluable manpower in a war of attrition, while playing a key role that helped to ensure the destruction of the Confederacy. The South failed to use its far greater availability of black manpower as soldiers. Ironically, the Confederacy was vanquished partly because it had refused to forsake slavery—the only way to have gained foreign recognition—and by not employing large numbers of black troops in gray uniforms until early 1865, when it was too late.

One of these black soldiers and former slaves who made the most of his newly-won freedom was Rappahannock County's Charles Davenport. He served in Colonel Robert Gould Shaw's 54th Massachusetts Volunteer Infantry that has been formed in the Boston, Massachusetts, area, in early 1863.

This fine regiment consisted of mostly free blacks from the North, as opposed to former slaves who dominated the ranks of almost all USCT regiments, won fame during the bloody assault on Fort Wagner, South Carolina, in July 1863 just outside Charleston. At this time, Charleston was one of the South's most strategic cities because of its vital links to the Atlantic and the outside world. Even more, Charleston was the home of secession that the revenge-seeking black soldiers especially desired to see captured for both symbolic and moral reasons.

Most important, Eliza and her fellow slaves on their Virginia plantation situated along the eastern edge of Rappahannock County amid the gently rolling terrain of the Blue Ridge foothills had early understood what the presence of large numbers of Union soldiers on Virginia soil would mean to them and their futures, if Abe Lincoln's boys moved into their home county in large numbers: the sweet taste of liberation that the slaves had dreamed about all their lives.[10]

Eliza's Final Escape

All the while, the winds of war continued to blow in the direction of Eliza and the Virginia Piedmont of northern Virginia during the summer of 1863, as if determined by fate and destiny. After the miserable failure of the Army of Northern Virginia's last bid to reap a dramatic victory on northern soil to "conquer a peace" and win the South's independence by way of a negotiated settlement during a war of attrition that it could never win, if the Army of the Potomac had been crushed at Gettysburg, Pennsylvania, on July 1-3, 1863, Lee's broken army escaped southward.

In the gloomiest of withdrawals in the pouring rain of July and after having crossed the Potomac River, Lee's troops retreated back into the safety of Virginia and the east side of the imposing Blue Ridge. Thanks in no small part to the efforts of Custer and his Michigan men who fought in the Union Army's rear and as noted, the repulse of "Pickett's Charge" ensured Lee's defeat at Gettysburg on the bloody third day, while sealing the Confederacy's fate and paving the way for the final drama to be played out at Appomattox

Court House on April 9, 1865. After the guns of Gettysburg had ceased to roar from July 1 to July 3, 1863, the brutal fighting in Virginia and the struggle for Richmond's possession was destined to continue for nearly two more years, however.

Hard-riding Union cavalry, including Custer's Second Brigade, Third Cavalry Division, attempted to intercept the retreat of Lee's Army out of the Shenandoah Valley, across the Blue Ridge, and into the Loudon Valley and the fertile lands of the Virginia Piedmont.

On July 24, Custer was ordered to advance ahead of the Major General George Gordon Meade's Army of the Potomac to gain Newly's Crossroads, situated four miles southwest of Amissville, where it was reported that Lee's column was located. Custer's troopers, including the hard-hitting Michigan Brigade, dashed through the picturesque countryside of the Piedmont to fulfill their mission and they shortly gained possession of the small agricultural community of Amissville, while hoping to follow-up on their remarkable success of July 3.

During the last week of July 1863, Custer's troopers began to skirmish with Lee's soldiers, who continued to withdraw down the eastern edge of Rappahannock County and just east of the Blue Ridge. While working as a slave at the main house, Eliza heard the crackle of gun-fire, mostly from fast-firing Union cavalry carbines, that rose higher in the steamy, summer air, indicating that the boys in blue were coming her way. Eliza, therefore, had begun to lay secret plans to escape the bonds of slavery and taste freedom for the first time in her life.

With confidence and faith that she could succeed in life once she escaped and then beginning life anew on her own, Eliza contemplated a new future as never before. By this time, Eliza was on her own. She had neither children or husband for whatever reason, and evidently due to slavery's imposed limitations and demands.

However, Eliza's mother was still living on the plantation, and this meant having to leave her mother behind on the plantation in rural Rappahannock County. It is not known, but Eliza's mother might have been sick or infirm because of an advanced age at this time, and she was unable to join her daughter in the daring escape attempt.

For pressing reasons, therefore, Eliza was going to leave the plantation alone and without her mother on a suitably dark night to avoid detection. Most important, Eliza was convinced that she could somehow survive entirely on her own and away from the close-knit community of slaves and even her kindly "ole Missus," who had provided her with food and shelter as long as she could remember almost like a real mother.

In late July 1863, Eliza, consequently, made the most important decision of her life, when she decided to take control of and seize her own destiny by departing the plantation. All in all, this was giant step forward for this young slave woman, and Eliza was determined to make it to freedom at any cost. She realized that it was time to take the considerable risk of attempting to escape slavery in a bold decision that she hoped would change her life forever, because the opportunity was now never better with Custer and his men so close.

With the sounds of skirmishing by Custer's troopers, that included the battle-hardened Michigan Wolverines, echoing over the Piedmont's rolling lands in late July, freedom beckoned to Eliza and it could no longer be resisted. The appeal of the sounds of the guns dominated Eliza's thoughts to fuel her aspirations and hopes, despite her relatively easy life in the "big house" compared to the dismal, mundane existence of the plantation's other slaves, who toiled in the fields of misery under the hot Virginia sun.

With no reservations or familial responsibilities or obligations that provided either an obstacle and burden because her mother was evidently not in need of her personal care, therefore, Eliza packed up her meager belongings from her quarters, which contained a common dirt floor and sparse furnishings, and extra food from a stockpiled supply in preparation for taking the greatest risk of her life. She made thorough preparations for leaving everything and fleeing the only home that she had ever known and her "ole Missus" by embarking upon a new life of freedom with high hopes.

Wearing her trademark bandana and calico dress, Eliza was now ready to boldly embrace the mysterious unknown that embodied an unprecedented amount of personal freedom for the first time in her life. Nevertheless, she was eager to take the challenge and to fully embrace the exciting prospects of a new life on her own and whatever that might be. Eliza knew that a host of new opportunities and possibilities lay in her future, although she did not know what they were at this time.

In her own words, Eliza described how the thrill of the high anticipation that had swept through the slave quarters on the Virginia plantation in the Virginia Piedmont, when the noisy racket of sharp skirmishing—a crackling sound in the distance that sounded like a Fourth of July celebration-- had reached new heights in the surrounding area: "everybody was excited over freedom, and I wanted to see how it was. Everybody keeps asking me why I left [the plantation]. I can't see why they can't recollect what war was for [the liberation of slaves], and that we were all bound to try and see for ourselves how it was."[11]

Clearly, in Eliza's mind and like for other slaves, the concept of freedom was something dear that was ever-so-precious, but still mysterious, while holding the potential to bring a bright, new day unlike anything that she had ever seen or known before in her life. Most of all, freedom had long tugged at Eliza's heart and soul. This heartfelt longing from deep inside of this young woman created a power pull and incentive to depart the plantation as soon as possible now that the golden opportunity had finally arrived in Rappahannock County.

The sweet taste of freedom was something that young Eliza had imagined and dreamed about for her entire life, and now that time was nearer than ever before. And thanks to the unexpected changes brought about by the sudden and unpredictable swirl of combat and because her home state of Virginia had been transformed into a major battleground in this bitter war over slavery and America's heart and soul, the golden opportunity now existed to escape the plantation to start anew in life, placing Eliza in a state of high anticipation in consequence.

Most important, Eliza would not allow the precious chance, with blue troopers under young Brigadier General George Armstrong Custer nearby, of a lifetime to slip by. Therefore, she knew that no time could be wasted because she had to escape the nightmare of slavery before it was too late.[12]

But in fact, the risk of attempting to escape was high for slaves, especially a young female, who were bold enough to take the risk in the depths of Rappahannock County, as elsewhere in Virginia and the South. For instance, when Wesley Norris and his family attempted to escape their slave-owner, Robert E. Lee, who now commanded the primary Southern Army in the Eastern Theater, the black family discovered that a cruel price had to be paid in full, if captured.

Knowing that harsh discipline was important in owning slaves and keeping them in a state of fear, even the gentlemanly and even-tempered Lee ordered a local sheriff "to strip us to the waist and give us fifty lashes each." All the while during this unfortunate ordeal, the aristocratic Lee "stood by, and frequently enjoined the constable to 'lay it on well," with the bullwhip. Even worse according to Norris, Lee ordered the use of saltwater "to thoroughly wash our backs" to intensify the pain in the harshest of punishments.[13]

However, taking the risk of attempting to escape and facing new dangers were necessary for Eliza and other Virginia slaves at this precious moment when Custer and his troopers were nearby and represented a safe haven, where misery and abuses ended forever: the price that had to be paid for seeking freedom.

In moving words that revealed her pain, Harriet Jacobs described her tragic experience when trapped in slavery when she was around Eliza's age: "I was twenty-one years in that cage of obscene birds. I can testify, from my own experience and observation, that slavery is a curse to the whites as well as to the blacks . . . And as far as the colored race, [no words can] describe the extremity of their suffering, the depth of their degradation."[14]

However, by this time when the gaining of freedom burned brightly, any fate was well worth the risk to Eliza, who had made up her mind, evidently on July 24, when young Brigadier General Custer, who had secured additional intelligence about the enemy's location from an escaped male slave on the night of July 23, and his men advanced and struck Lee's withdrawing column.

Custer had been ordered to gain the strategic position known as Newly's Crossroads, where the main road led south to Culpeper, Virginia, (around 35 miles slightly northwest of Fredericksburg, Virginia) when he had collided with elements of General Ambrose Powell Hill's Third Corps, Army of Northern Virginia. Born in Virginia and a capable West Pointer, the hard-fighting Hill was one of Lee's finest top lieutenants. Hill was fated not to survive the war, falling just outside Petersburg, Virginia, near the war's end.

In a hotly-contested clash of arms known as Battle Mountain, Custer's bluecoat troopers of the Second Brigade skirmished with Lee's troops around the vicinity of Newly's Crossroads. This dusty crossroads in the middle of nowhere was located around four miles southwest of Amissville and just five miles south of the stately Ben Venue mansion built in 1844, the row of rustic slave quarters, and crossroads and southeast of where Eliza had been born.

But, of course, the Ben Venue Crossroads was not the only key intersection in eastern Rappahannock County that was destined to become a bone of contention for marching armies engaged in the art of maneuver across the Piedmont, when the bluecoats were focused on cutting off Lee's line of retreat deeper into the Old Dominion.

Newly's Crossroads had been named after the Newly family, which had early settled in this part of the Virginia Piedmont. From this quiet, tidy village, nestled amid a pastoral countryside of rolling hills, that was smaller than Amissville, determined men in gray and butternut uniforms had first marched off to war in the South's defense during the spring of 1861. These young men and boys who fought for their beloved Virginia were highly-motivated fighters, and quite a few of them now lay in shallow graves scattered across Virginia.

However, since that heady time during the spring of 1861 when it had seemed that anything was possible for Southerners in arms, other men of a darker hue and equal determination had also gone forth to wage their own personal war against slavery. For instance, William Newly became a member of the 5th United States Colored Troops, putting on the blue uniform and serving with pride.

He was destined to be mortally wounded in the fighting at Petersburg, Virginia, in the bloody year of 1864. Part of the group of former slaves of the wealthy Newly family for which the crossroads had been named, he was the brother of Virginia-born Dangerfield Newly, the oldest of John Brown's raiders and one of the first freedom-loving men who had been killed in the attack on Harpers Ferry, of Rappahannock County.[15]

Meanwhile, as Eliza listened to the sounds of combat in the distance, the spattering of gun-fire, especially the roar of the rapid-fire .52 caliber Spencer repeating rifles of Custer's veteran troopers, rose higher on this hot morning of July 24. The sharp crackle of the musketry revealed the extent of the fighting that raged in the summer heat, signaling to Eliza that it was finally time to depart.

Indeed, the sound of the firing told Eliza and other slaves that the Yankees were now even closer–just four miles southwest of Amissville. To the anxious Eliza, she now knew that this time was her long-awaited opportunity to escape. However, as noted, considerable risks remained for a female slave on her own, and Eliza had not made her final decision lightly largely because she would have to leave her mother behind on the plantation that she called home.

Not unlike at the East Cavalry Field in the Union Army's rear on July 3, Custer had encountered a larger number of Confederates in Rappahannock County than he had anticipated. The young brigadier general even feared that he had run into the entire corps under Lee's best top lieutenant, James Longstreet, who led the crack troops of the First Corps, Army of Northern Virginia. As Custer had later learned, the battle-hardened veterans of the First Corps had been the primary attackers during Pickett's Charge that had targeted Meade's right-center on Cemetery Ridge.

Facing overwhelming numbers and on the verge of being out-flanked by Hill's Third Corps infantry, therefore, Custer prudently retired his troopers from the vicinity of the dusty roads of Newly Crossroads and the around four miles northeast toward Amissville. The fight was sharp and close-range, but losses were relatively light for Custer's cavalrymen. Here, at Amissville, the young brigadier general concentrated his far-flung cavalry units of the Second Brigade, Third Division, to await future developments in case the Confederates continued to display aggressiveness and even advanced to once again engage the boys in blue.[16]

After the lengthy skirmish that had almost evolved into a full-scale battle before he had ordered his men to fall back, Custer encamped his forces at Amissville. Here, he planned to concentrate his troopers and to weigh future tactical options based on the most recent accurate intelligence that could be gained by him. Weary Union troopers, covered in dust and sweat, basked in the respite at Amissville.

Custer had made his headquarters in a modest two-story house located about a mile just southeast of the small village of Amissville. Here, Custer's cavalry command remained for the next ten days, recuperating from their most arduous campaign to date, while Lee's Army slipped farther away, since the fighting was now over. Both men and horses of

Custer's Michigan Brigade required rest and recuperation, especially after the three bloodiest days in American history in Adams County, Pennsylvania.

In addition, foragers in blue needed to range throughout the rich, unspoiled countryside in this part of the Northern Virginia Piedmont, which had escaped the ravages of war, to gather provisions for the always hungry troopers, including the Michigan Wolverines, who were Custer's boys and favorites, and forage for their mounts.

For the first time in months, Custer's men finally gained some much-needed rest, having earned the long-awaited respite that bestowed the opportunity which allowed large numbers of Rappahannock County slaves to escape slavery and gain the refuge of Custer's command. Eliza was about to become one of these successful escapees.

In this small, plain house, with a wide front porch and solid stone foundation, that had been built in 1860, Custer settled down at a table to write intelligence reports for General Meade about his recent activities, observations, and what intelligence that he had gained from having encountered Lee's troops on the morning of July 24 and from the knowledge of escaped slaves, who had flooded into Amissville to greet their liberators.

To the black escapees, it seemed as if these Yankees had been heaven-sent, despite their rough looks, dirty uniforms, unkept beards, and hardened veteran's demeanor. After all, the Michigan troopers had been through hell and back on the bloody third day at Gettysburg, while following the ever-energetic Custer who always led from the front.

In late July, Eliza was just another one of the Rappahannock County slaves who was destined to eventually to reach Custer's command at Amissville. This small town was yet another neat, tidy rural community nestled in the scenic Blue Ridge foothills. It is not known, but Eliza might have previously seen this place while a slave in the past.[17]

As she explained the situation and her reasoning at this time when Custer and his troopers were encamped near the plantation on which Eliza had long worked: "After the 'Mancipation [by President Abraham Lincoln on January 1 1863], everybody was a-standin' up for liberty, and I wasent goin' to stay home when everybody else was a-goin'."[18]

During the last week of July after slipping through the cool shadows of the hardwood forests of the Virginia Piedmont, Eliza finally reached Custer's main encampment at Amissville. In her own words that described the turning point of her life, "I jined the Ginnel at Amosville [Amissville], Rappahannock County, in August, 1863."[19]

Here, Eliza found a good many other slaves who also had escaped their masters in the local area. No doubt, she knew some of the other escapees, especially if they had come from her own plantation. She explained how, "The [late July] day I came into camp, there was a good many other darkeys from all about our place."[20]

The Most Fortunate of Meetings

At this time, the sense of liberation and freedom was immensely intoxicating for Eliza, because the arrival of a bright new day was in the air. She had never been around so many black and white people before in one place, while basking in her new-found freedom.

At the small town in the Virginia Piedmont, Eliza also saw the steeple of the wooden Methodist Church, where Southern volunteers, including members of the Amiss family who had founded the community, had once drilled to the orders of the town's fiery preacher, who was secessionist to the core. Like so many other men of this town, so this revered man of God had then gone to war as a holy warrior in a gray uniform.

Eliza now became part of the throng of blacks, who had been recently liberated from Rappahannock County and neighboring counties like Warren, Madison, Fauquier and two others in this part of the Piedmont. These black escapees had been attaching themselves to Custer's command since July 23. For the newly-liberated blacks, including Eliza, it almost seemed as if these white men in blue uniforms were guardian angels and disciples of the Lord.

At the contraband camp located either in the little town of Amissville or near Custer's headquarters in the modest residence located just to the southeast, Eliza first saw General Custer which was a sight that she would never forget. Only age twenty-three, he had only recently benefitted from a dramatic rise in his fortunes. Custer had been appointed to a brigadier general's rank on June 28, 1863 and only days before the Battle of Gettysburg, where he had played a leading role in saving the day for the Union during the crucial showdown on the East Cavalry Field on the final day of decision.[21]

Among a group of liberated slaves from the local area, Eliza never forgot the moment when she saw the handsome, well-built, and dashing General Custer, now only age twenty-three and in his physical prime: "We was a-standin' round waitin' when I first seed the Ginnel."[22]

With a natural eye for feminine beauty of all colors and especially if a slim and physically fit young woman which was his distinct preference since his youth as later on in life, Custer saw Eliza first, when he "approached" this attractive, dark-skinned young woman on his own initiative. Custer approached her in his typical bold manner "among the band of runaways and [eventually] asked her if she would serve in the position" as a cook and laundress for himself and his headquarters staff of young officers.

Flattered by the offer and with a golden opportunity having presented itself when least expected from a full-fledged general of the United States Army, Eliza readily consented when it seemed as if destiny and fate itself had deemed it so.[23]

From now on after she uttered the words "I reckon I would" in response to the young brigadier general's request for her to join him and his staff as a cook and laundress, Eliza's fate was linked to Custer not only for the rest of the Civil War, but also for the next six years.

As could be expected, however, young Eliza naturally missed her mother and the close-knit slave community that she had just departed forever, feeling a sense of guilt for having left them behind, while she now basked in the opportunity that Custer had presented to her and one that was well beyond her wildest expectations.

Eliza had never previously been away from her mother and the insular world of the slave community. In her own words, Eliza described how: "But, oh, how awful lonesome I was at fust, and I was afraid of everything in the shape of war. I used to wish myself back on the old plantation with my mother."[24]

Under the circumstances, this fear was entirely understandable and natural given the fact that Eliza was away from her mother and the slave community, including friends and perhaps other relatives, for the first time in her life and this was her first experience in a wartime environment. At this time, she had never seen so many white soldiers before or so many firearms in one place, and Eliza felt the wonder of it all.

And, of course, Eliza had also never previously seen the cannon of the horse artillery that accompanied Custer's troopers and protected them in the heat of combat. War was an entirely new experience for Eliza and she would never be the same, after having decided to link her destiny with this young brigadier general and his staff of equally young men of promise.

But in the absence of her family, someone else was shortly destined to fill the gaping void that had been left in Eliza's personal and emotional life and to ease the sorrow that she felt for the first time in having been away from home and her mother: a young man whose star was still on the rise after his rendezvous with destiny at Gettysburg on the decisive afternoon of July 3, General George Armstrong Custer.[25]

Chapter II

Fury of The Civil War Years

Quite unknown to her at the time, when Eliza made the personal choice to cast her fate and fortunes with this young, long-haired white man in a resplendent blue uniform of a brigadier general, she could not have possibly imagined what her decision entailed in regard to future risks and dangers when she had agreed, as Custer's own request, to join him as a cook and laundress. A novice of all things military and war, this was new kind of world—the Army of the Potomac—that Eliza knew nothing about.

Ironically, she almost certainly would not have accepted Custer's offer had she known of the stern challenges and trials, especially the full extent of the dangers, that lay ahead. Custer was destined to become the hardest-fighting Union cavalry officer of the war, winning repeated laurels, and establishing a sterling combat record that was second to no other Union cavalry general from 1864-1865. And Eliza would be with him during key moments of this most impressive career that made Custer into one of the Union's greatest heroes across the North, before the fighting finally mercifully ceased.

During this crucial period when America's fate was decided in the war's final campaigns in her own home state of Virginia, Eliza's life was often in danger, and she was nearly captured more than once. In fact, she was briefly captured by the Rebels during a close call at the Battle of Trevilian Station on June 11, 1864, when Custer and his Michigan Brigade were surrounded in "Custer's First Last Stand" and the general's personal possessions and baggage train was captured by Virginia cavalrymen.

Much was at stake for Eliza in joining the boys in blue. Of course, permanent capture by the Rebels would have meant the worst of all fates for Eliza: a quick return to a miserable life in slavery, perhaps even suffering the fate of a public sale on the auction block at a sizeable Southern town like Richmond, the Confederacy's capital city, or Petersburg just to the south.

But all in all, when Eliza decided to join Custer at his headquarters for a period of service that was destined to last for years, she was about to enter the most exciting, adventurous, and eventful period of her life. After all, Eliza was about to become a veteran campaigner in following Custer and one of the hard-fighting combat units of the Army of the Potomac across wide stretches of Virginia.

As mentioned, for escaped slaves like Eliza, no fate could have been worse than capture by the Confederates. An understanding West Pointer and Pennsylvania-born General Horace Porter, who served in the Army of the Potomac and was attended by black servants at headquarters, recalled that whenever Lee's seemingly invincible troops attacked and often without warning, "The black boys [servants and former slaves who were attending Union officers in camp] were not to be blamed for manifesting fright, for they all had a notion that their lives would not be worth paying for if they fell into the hands of the enemy and were recognized as persons who had made their escape from slavery to serve in the Yankee army."[26]

Therefore, at Amissville upon first joining Custer, Eliza never fully realized that the risks of serving with this young commander would be so high. However, she almost certainly knew that there would be dangers that lay ahead for her since this was an unpredictable military environment. Eliza, nevertheless, embraced Custer's challenge instead of deciding to flee across Northern Virginia to reach Pennsylvania just to the north, where she would be safe not only from having entered free territory for the first time in her life, but also she would have been farther away from a war that was growing more brutal with each passing day.[27]

From the beginning and playing their part as liberators, Custer and his men had welcomed the escaped slaves throughout the final week of July, sharing their food, mainly hardtack, with the escaped blacks, including a good many women and children who were now on their own.

From these fortunate escapees, including perhaps Eliza, Custer gained information about Lee's latest movements, intentions, and strength. At this time and to his credit, Custer referred to blacks as negroes at a time when many northern soldiers used much less flattering names, to say the least, in their letters and diaries for the newly-freed blacks.

In his official correspondence as written from the small town of Amissville in Rappahannock County and within sight of the bluish-colored ridges of the Blue Ridge Mountains that loomed on the western horizon, Custer also referred to the escaped slaves as "contrabands." Because the United States Fugitive Slave Law of 1850—part of the United States Constitution that had caused outrage across the North since having been first enacted--required the return of escaped slaves to owners and this pro-slavery national legislation was the law of the land, escaped slaves who had fled to Union Armies had early required a new legal classifications and definition.

Therefore, to circumvent the national law that was now a pressing necessary in wartime, General Benjamin Butler, a gifted and experienced Massachusetts lawyer, deemed that the escaped Virginia slaves who had fled to his lines at Fort Monroe, on the Virginia Peninsula, southeast of Richmond, were to be legally defined as "contraband of war." With this new legal classification to meet wartime requirements, the escaped slaves, including Eliza, were then legally retained by Union forces and officially put to work for the Union army and cause.

Exploiting General Butler's clever legal loophole, the United States Congress then passed the First Confiscation Act to support Butler's novel contraband concept, which became a legal reality during the summer of 1861. Then, in July 1862 and thankfully for escaped slaves, the Second Confiscation Act was passed by Congress, which proclaimed that all contrabands who gained the Union lines were "forever free." [28]

In consequence, Eliza Denison Brown officially and legally became a "contraband" and "forever free," when she had entered Union lines around or at Amissville on either

July 23, 24, or 25, where Custer's headquarters was located.[29]

As noted, some of these escaped slaves had brought vital intelligence to Custer at an early date. On July 23, for example, Custer described how, "Since dark, a contraband has come in from Newly's Cross-Roads with very reliable information. He reports the enemy moving hurried by Newly's Cross-Roads on the Culpeper [Virginia] road [and] The negro says it is [Ambrose Powell] Hill's corps."[30]

Then, in the early afternoon of July 25, Custer penned another report from his Amissville headquarters to his superior, Major General Alfred Pleasonton, a talented West Pointer, who had been born in Washington, D.C., which might well have pertained partly to information relayed by Eliza, if she had acquired any such intelligence during her desperate flight to link with Union troops: "From citizens and contrabands living in the vicinity of Gaines' Cross-Roads, I learned that my attack on Newly's Cross-Roads spread great consternation through the entire rebel column, extending beyond Gaines' in the direction of Chester Gap."[31]

Almost certainly and besides the longing for freedom that stirred her soul to have fueled her escape from slavery's horrors, Eliza felt a sense of duty and obligation to serve the soldiers in blue, who were the revered saviors of her people.

Indeed, wherever the Union troops went in the South with muskets on shoulders, they freed the slaves along the way. Therefore, the Yankees were viewed as Mr. Lincoln's saintly liberators by freed blacks, who rejoiced in their golden days of Jubilee.[32]

Now finally freed from slavery for the first time in her life, Eliza embarked upon her new responsibilities at Custer's headquarters with not only enthusiasm, but also with a zeal. Naturally, she early wanted to prove her worth to herself and Custer, while supporting the boys in blue as much as possible.

In her role as a cook, laundress, and general organizer of Custer's headquarters of young officers who needed a degree of maternal supervision when it came to their domestic matters, Eliza came into her own as never before. And from the beginning, Eliza's efforts were greatly appreciated by Custer and the members of his talented staff of the Second Cavalry Brigade, when they were on campaign and in the field.

This new life for her at Custer's headquarters was the great opportunity that Eliza had seemingly been made for and had been awaiting all her life. For the first time and with her spirit soaring without having to answer to and mindlessly obey her Rappahannock County owners and other white

Southerners, Eliza eagerly proved her abilities and skills to one and all month after month during arduous campaigns across Virginia.

All the while, Eliza continued feel a good deal of loyalty and devotion to the boys in blue and especially Custer, who gave her a great opportunity to shine as a person like never before in her life. To Eliza and as mentioned, these young men and boys, who hailed from places that she had never seen or heard about before, were her God-given liberators, and Custer symbolized all that was good about the soldiers of Mr. Lincoln's liberating armies.

For ample good reason, Eliza Dennison Brown was indeed thankful to her lucky stars because this was indeed the opportunity of a lifetime in serving Custer and his staff and she clearly made the most of it during the remainder of the war's course.

Indeed, when by Custer's side and working for him and the general's personal staff of his cavalry brigade and then his division of the Army of the Potomac, Eliza truly came into her own. She excelled in all manner of duties, including the supervision of other domestic supporters (former slaves, male and female) of the general's staff and many of the staff's functions, while in the army's encampment.

A Young Man on the Rise

After Eliza joined Custer, the young man's career was nothing less than meteoric during the bloody years of 1864 and 1865. Beginning in 1864, Lieutenant General Ulysses S. Grant led his Army of the Potomac south toward Richmond during the Overland Campaign. He now commanded all Union forces, thanks to his winning ways first in the Western Theater and then in the Eastern Theater, thanks to President Lincoln's sage judgment. All the while, Custer continued to rise to the fore. Grant now pushed south in a bid to capture Richmond with overpowering resources and manpower.

Then, Custer and his cavalry command served later in New York-born General Philip Sheridan's Army in the Shenandoah Valley, where victory in the fall of 1864 was achieved in the Confederacy's most strategic valley, which had long served as the breadbasket of the Army of Northern Virginia. Both of these campaigns that helped to place the Confederacy on the road to destruction were conducted in Eliza's home state.

Then, Custer led his cavalry division of hard-hitting troopers with his usual skill and distinction during the Appomattox Campaign of early 1865. Custer's cavalrymen played a key role in harassing and blocking Lee's retreat west from Petersburg with what little was left of the reeling Army of Northern Virginia, which had been thoroughly decimated by desertions and attrition. Lee's battered army was finally forced to surrender on a glorious Palm Sunday, April 9, 1865 at Appomattox, Virginia.

In consequence, Custer emerged as one of the greatest of the North's heroes, because he possessed the winning touch. Throughout the arduous campaigns, long marches, rains and snows, and seemingly endless skirmishers and battles, Eliza remained with Custer and his staff, doing her duties in support of the Union war effort.

Incredibly, by the war's end, Custer was a rising star second to none in the Army of the Potomac's cavalry corps and his promise seemed without limit: hence, the shock that shook America to the core when the nation's most famous and boldest cavalier met his inglorious end at the hands of Sioux and Cheyenne warriors on a hot late June afternoon in 1876.

With the war's conclusion during the spring of 1865, the victorious Union armies of the eastern theater marched to Washington, D.C., for the much-awaited victory parade of around 150,000 troops in total down the broad width of Pennsylvania Avenue. Therefore, with Sheridan's troops and as part of Custer's headquarters, Eliza was also with Custer in the nation's capital near the end of May 1865, after Lee's surrender at Appomattox. Unlike Custer, this was the first time that this former slave from Rappahannock County, Virginia, had seen the nation's capital. She must have marveled at the sights and the Washington Monument, which was still under construction and only about half-completed at this time.

Here, like across the North, all Washington, D.C. was celebrating its great victory over the Confederacy, which was no more after having been relegated to the ash heap of history. First, Grant's 90,000-man Army of the Potomac on May 23 and then William T. Sherman's 60,000-man Army of the Tennessee on May 24, prepared for the northern military's "last great spectacle." Two tough westerners and kindred spirits, Generals Grant and Sherman formed the hard-hitting top leadership team that had brought decisive Union victory in the end.

On May 23 and in the neat formations of hardened veterans, the proud fighting men of the triumphant Army of the Potomac marched down the length of Pennsylvania Avenue, while crowds cheered wildly during the nation's "most imposing [celebration] in its history."[33].

At this time, Eliza yet attended Custer, and she witnessed the grand review in the festive mood that dominated the nation's capital. If so, then she also saw Custer's grandstanding because he seemingly made the most of every opportunity like on the battlefield.

In the words of General Horace Porter, a West Pointer who had won a Medal of Honor for his heroics in the Civil War (like Custer's younger brother, Thomas "Tom" Custer, who won two of the nation's highest awards during the critical first week of April 1865 and he was fated to die at the Little Bighorn on June 25, 1876), who described how during the review Custer once again stole the show, before the eyes of President Lincoln, leading officials, and the exciting throng: "Conspicuous among the division commanders was Custer. His long golden locks floating in the wind, his low-cut collar, his crimson necktie, and his buckskin breeches, presented a combination which made him look half general and half scout, and gave him a daredevil appearance. When within two hundred yards of the President's [reviewing] stand, his spirited horse took the bit in his teeth, and made a dash past the troops, rushing by the reviewing offices like a tornado; but he found more than a match in Custer, and was soon checked, and forced back to his proper position."[34]

If Eliza, who was known for her sharp wit and biting sense of humor, had teased Custer about his sleeping in the rain and the undeniable fact that he had "wanted Miss Libbie with you" as a love-making companion in the dreary downpour, then she would have almost certainly joked about his wild ride past President Lincoln during the grand review.[35]

On May 23, General "Little Phil" Sheridan had been given a new assignment to the Texas border and the Rio Grande River country by General Grant, because of French intervention in Mexico in violation of the Monroe Doctrine, after these European interlopers taken full advantage of the opportunity with the United States self-destructing from 1861-1865. Sheridan headed for Brownsville, Texas with around 50,000 troops when the possibility of having to engage in another war, while the rest of the Army of Potomac was mustered out of service during the systematic dismantling of the North's great war machine.

However, the conflict was over for the vast majority of Grant's and Sherman's troops who laid down their arms and mustered out of service. Custer and Eliza never forgot the magnificent sight of the grand review. Seasoned veterans who had been part of the famous "March to the Sea" that had cut a destructive swath through the heart of Georgia,

General Sherman's men proudly represented the western army during the grand review.[36]

Custer's enlistment in the United States Army expired in March 1866. Consequently, he was officially mustered out of service as a major general of volunteers in Washington, D.C. in early March. Despite having been one of the North's greatest Civil War heroes and much to his disappointment and that of spendthrift Elizabeth, Custer's pay was cut by three-fourths when his rank reverted back to its prewar level of a lowly captain in the regular army like when a young officer fresh out of West Point in 1861.

With Custer now having only a small government allowance for living expenses, Elizabeth had been already sent home to her family of her father judge in Monroe. At this time and nearly a year after the war's end, Eliza remained by Custer's side, sharing his fate and destiny in peacetime like during the war years.

Instead of leaving Custer and the army, Eliza had remained with him on her own free will, because she believed in the value of loyalty and faithfulness like Custer. Even more for other personal reasons, she decided not to leave like other civilian blacks, especially those liberated from slavery, who had attached themselves as domestic workers to Union Armies during the war years across the

South and to many Federal officers of all ranks. Most of all and through all the ups and downs, Eliza was supremely devoted to Custer and never wavered.[37]

Meanwhile and as noted, Custer and Eliza stayed together in the nation's capital after the awe-inspiring display of the grand review, while Libbie was living with her family in Monroe. With the war's end and after the devastation that had been inflicted on Virginia by invading Union armies, Eliza was concerned about the welfare of her former master, an older woman who had treated her kindly throughout the past.

Of course, such a level of deep concern displayed Eliza's big heart for a Southern woman who might have been a Confederate sympathizer, which was most likely the case unless she had been born in the North. However, Eliza never forgot the kindness that this Southern white woman had been shown in the past by her elderly master who had managed without a husband, thanks to Eliza's invaluable assistance.

On March 16, 1866, therefore, Custer wrote a letter to Elizabeth in Monroe to inform his wife that he had allowed his faithful free woman to color to proceed on her mission west that Eliza had deemed as all-important to her in personal terms: "Eliza has gone to visit her 'old Missus' [and] She will then start for Monroe."[38]

Despite the war's end and as noted, Eliza remained with Custer because she was part of the Custer "family" after the war, displaying her faithfulness and despite the fact that the men of Custer's staff had been mustered out of service. After all, by this time and as mentioned, she had developed an extremely close relationship with Custer and his wife, because they had become her surrogate family. However, Eliza could not completely separate herself from the slave past and what that had meant to her before Custer had married Elizabeth in early 1864.

On her own and although few details are known about the journey and as mentioned, consequently, Eliza had returned to her last home of her "old Missus" in Northern Virginia, after traveling west on her own across a war-torn countryside. As noted, her mother (unfortunately, her name is unknown) had remained on the plantation in Rappahannock County, when Eliza had escaped from slavery to join Custer in late July 1863. Custer had given her sufficient funds and his best wishes for the journey to former homeland of Northern Virginia to make sure that Eliza's elderly female master was doing fine.

Eliza's trek back to where she had been a slave in Rappahannock County in the Virginia Piedmont no doubt brought back a flood of memories (good and bad), emotions, and strong feelings, revealing the complexities of the slave experience in all varieties. In many ways, Eliza was a passionate young woman of strong emotions, which explained her devotion not only to Custer but also her elderly former owner.

Most of all, she wanted to see her mother, who had survived the Civil War years. While she still very liked her "old Missus" because of her past kindness, Eliza had naturally felt a deep hatred toward the institution of slavery and the pre-Civil War laws of the American nation and the State of Virginia that had kept her in a permanent bondage for which there seemed no escape until Custer's arrival.

It was quite obvious that Eliza, who remained open-minded in matters of race, held no grudges against her former female master and other white Southerners, knowing that they in truth had been almost as much victims of America's most insidious institution as blacks in the end. In this sense and as Eliza saw it, her "old Missus" was neither guilty or culpable in the creation of the great sin of slavery and she acted accordingly.

This common sense attitude of the thoughtful former slave from Rappahannock County has provided additional proof that Eliza was "sage," in Custer's words, beyond her years to have internalized as much in regard to slavery and its detrimental effects on whites in the long term. She fully understood that both the people of the North and South had been equally guilty of having perpetuated America's greatest national sin to reap ill-gained profits, because they had mutually benefitted from slavery for generations.[39]

But if Eliza believed that she had seen the last of military life and war when General Lee surrendered his army at Appomattox Court House on Palm Sunday 1865, then she was sadly mistaken. While she was visiting her former master in Northern Virginia amid the familiar confines of Rappahannock County, Custer had been busy in Washington, D.C. , after he had decided to continue his military career rather than resign and try his luck in civilian life with all of its uncertainties. As Custer penned in a March 18, 1866 letter: "I procured [an] appointment to the regular army, from Sec'y [Edwin M.] Stanton."[40]

Of course and as a cruel fate would have it, Custer had no idea that the eagerly-sought appointment that he had gained to his delight all but ensured that he was destined to become an Indian fighter and meet a tragic end on the distant Northern Great Plains at the Little Bighorn. However, Custer was most of all a soldier, and he had discovered that his true talents and skills lay in the art of war, which he had excelled at like few other Americans.

Meanwhile, after having visited her mother in Rappahannock County and "ole Missus," in her own words as related to Elizabeth by Custer in his March 16, 1866 letter, Eliza then proceeded on the nearly 500-mile journey northwest by rail to Elizabeth's hometown of Monroe, Michigan, on her own. Along the way, she saw a pristine land, the sprawling fields and woodlands of the North and the Midwest, that she had never seen before. This was the first time in her life that Eliza had been outside of her home state of Virginia and she basked in a degree of freedom and mobility that she had never known before.[41]

As already realized by Eliza and as noted, her life would never be the same after she had cast her destiny with one of America's greatest war heroes and "joined up with the Ginnil," in her own words, back in late July 1863 more than a year and a half before. However, while riding the rails across country to a new place, Monroe, Michigan, that she had never seen before, Eliza might have reflected upon the twisting, unpredictable course of her life and her fate.

In fact, Eliza very likely never imagined that she would soon be going even farther west and to an even stranger land when she would be once again by the side of Custer, who would shortly wage war against the Great Plains tribes in obeying orders from his government to subdue the unruly

Native Americans, who blocked the relentless push of settlement toward the Pacific.[42]

However, facing hard conditions, a rough life, and even existing in an environment of a hostile opponent were experiences that were hardly anything new to Eliza. Therefore, with a level of respect and admiration that rarely, if ever, existed between a famous general and a former slave, Custer had been quite correct by writing with admiration in a letter to Elizabeth on June 21, 1864: "Poor Eliza, faithful to the last!"[43]

Custer was right on target with his analysis about a person who might well have been described as his black soul mate for a variety of reasons. Eliza Brown was as loyal and as faithful to Custer as a good wife. He, therefore, considered her part of the family—a cherished, valued, and faithful member. Because she had seen her husband's own devotion and admiration for Eliza, Elizabeth perhaps felt jealousy to some degree at some point. If so, then this situation might well explain why Eliza was now on her way by rail to Monroe and Elizabeth and farther away from Custer who had remained back east at Washington, D.C.

After all, Custer and Eliza had been alone together quite a bit and through thick and thin from 1864 to 1865, which was perhaps too much as far as Elizabeth was concerned.

It is not known, but Elizabeth might well have grown somewhat uneasy about her husband's deep attachment to Eliza that seemed to be growing stronger over time.

Chapter III

The Great Plains and the Indian Wars

After the Civil War and the demobilization of the gigantic armies of the Union that had systematically vanquished the Confederacy and its armies during a brutal war of attrition, America now faced its greatest challenge out west. The historic push of the American people into the sprawling expanses of the West now continued after the four years of bloodletting of the brother's war: all part of one of the great human migrations in world history that had begun since before America's birth.

Consequently, the tens of thousands of settlers, including many Civil War veterans who desired to take advantage of the Homestead Act of 1862, were on the move toward the setting sun. They trekked west into the vastness of the Great Plains and needed protection from the United States military.

Likewise, the Kansas Pacific Railroad possessed the ambitious plan to push into central Kansas from Fort Riley,

Kansas, and all the way to the Pacific. Therefore, the expanding railroads and accompanying civilians, especially the workers and commercial interests, needed to be protected by the United States Army during the ambitious push westward.

Now new towns of optimistic and ambitious transplanted citizens sprang up like wildflowers in a rainy spring across the Great Plains, especially along the iron rails that were steadily being laid over the grasslands by multi-ethnic work gangs toward the Pacific.[44]

During the postwar period, Fort Riley, located on the north bank of the Kansas River, was the first assignment of the Custer family, including Eliza. In the fall of 1866, Libbie, Custer, and Eliza rode the rails of the Kansas Pacific Railroad west for the new assignment on the eastern edge of the Great Plains. Custer had been appointed the commander of the 7th Cavalry with the rank of lieutenant colonel near the end of July 1866. Fort Riley now served as the headquarters of the newly-formed 7th Cavalry, which included many former Civil War veterans.

In a letter that revealed her aristocratic roots and sentiments which were the antithesis of Eliza's more common views that were vastly different, Libbie described the quality service of black porters who attended to her whims to her first cousin, Rebecca Richmond of Grand Rapids, Michigan, "Oh, the Pacific R.R. is such a grand affair–the care are beautiful."[45]

On October 16, 1866, Custer, Libbie, and Eliza reached Fort Riley that was located on the muddy Kansas (also known as the Kaw) River situated west of Kansas City, Missouri, after making the long trip west of around 500 miles by rail from St. Louis to the open grasslands of north central Kansas.

Here, at the frontier fort located on the wide prairie of the eastern Great Plains, the new-comers, including Eliza, settled into a large stone, two-story structure of the officer's quarters. In her December 6, 1866 letter, Libbie basked in the good fortune of finding such excellent living quarters available to the commander of the 7th Cavalry and his wife.

Of course, this sentiment was also a view shared by Eliza, who also lived in the same house at Fort Riley because she was assigned to doing the domestic chores for the Custer family: "We are so much more comfortably situated here than we were at Winchester [Virginia, when Custer had been serving under General Sheridan during the 1864 Shenandoah Campaign]. The climate of Kansas is very fine, so pure and free from dampness. As yet we have not had a week of cold weather altogether."[46]

The Custer's family's quarters exceeded expectations of what they had expected of soldier life on the frontier. A true blueblood who was a novice to the frontier like her husband, Libbie had harbored serious misgivings about the anticipated quality of life and the assumed subpar officer's quarters that existed on the western frontier. In consequence, Elizabeth and Eliza had expected the worst during the westward journey to Fort Riley, which they had not seen before.

In the end, therefore, the Custer "family," including Eliza, were pleasantly surprised by what they found at the frontier fort, which was seemingly located in the middle of nowhere on the grassy prairie lands. As Libbie penned in her letter about the good life at Fort Riley: "We are living almost in luxury. It does not seem [like] life in the army for you know I have had mostly a rough time. This is not a fort, tho' called so, it is a garrison. For there are no walls enclosing it!"[47]

Clearly, Libbie, and no doubt Eliza, had good cause for concern about their own safety, when they envisioned the horror of a possible Indian attack on Fort Riley. Although Custer commanded the 7th Cavalry which was much different in terms of the overall quality of troopers compared to the men of his beloved Michigan regiments from Civil War days, Libbie and Eliza had never lived before on the frontier, ensuring that they had initially expected the worst.

At this time, capture by Native American raiders was the most serious of all concerns for women, black or white.

After all, one of the most pervasive white stereotypes was that Native American males sexually abused captive white women, which was actually not the case in almost all cases going back to colonial days—most of all, they were warriors with their own distinct and strict code of ethos, value systems, and not wild Great Plains rapists as generally thought at the time by whites. And, of course, the standard of beauty among Native American males failed to include white women and sexual abuses were minimized by the lack of attractiveness of white women in their eyes, as deemed by their cultural tastes and societal values.

Nevertheless, Elizabeth and Eliza were worried about their lives and the future that now looked bleak at an unprotected fort on the open plains. Indeed, if Native American raiders suddenly attacked Fort Riley, there were no walls or timbered palisade of the usual vertical logs to keep out a mounted raiding party, which might strike at any time. Of course at this time, the reputations of the ferocity of Native American warriors, including Cheyenne Dog Soldiers, were well-known to whites, especially women, who had grown to fear them to an excessive degree.

Such was the confidence and arrogance of the United States military establishment and its leaders, who were mostly Civil War veterans, that Fort Riley was completely vulnerable to attack. As mentioned, Elizabeth and Eliza certainly expressed their concerns upon first setting sight on Fort Riley, which was entirely unprotected in the traditional sense.[48]

However, there was more for the newcomers to worry about than possible threats from local tribes, because the task of moving so far west to the new Custer family quarters, located next to the commander's house, had been most demanding from the beginning. The fact that the quarters at Fort Riley for the famous leader of the 7th Cavalry exceeded their previously low expectations had placed both Libbie and Eliza, who would live with the couple, in an overall good mood and this bode well for the future of living and surviving in the West.

As Libbie described the housing arrangements in her December 6, 1866 letter to her first cousin, "The houses [of the officers] all have wide verandas [and] Our house has a large parlor, my bedroom back of it and dressing room next to that at the end of the hall. We have a back entry and Eliza's room at the rear."[49]

Libbie, or Elizabeth, became ecstatic about the new quarters and life on the Great Plains, enjoying a novel experience for the first time. As she continued in her December 6 letter to first cousin Rebecca back in Grand Rapids, Michigan, and despite still thralled over the "elegant time" recently spent in St. Louis that she described with enthusiasm and in detail: "So, you see, we are comfortable. I have a carpet on my bedroom also and expect to have one on the dressing-room. Eliza never did better than now."[50]

Besides an urban product dominated by an upper-class perspective and privileged ways as the judge's pampered daughter, Libbie's words revealed how Eliza was much more than a typical servant or domestic. She was not only like a family member but also more like an experienced chief organizer or manager of the Custer family affairs rather than a traditional lowly domestic: fundamental reasons why she was so highly admired by Custer year after year and since not long after the Battle of Gettysburg.

Indeed, Eliza's postwar role with the Custer family was basically much the same as it had been for Custer and his headquarters staff during the war years. Most of all, she was doer with a can-do attitude and spirit that never wavered, even in crisis situations that were encountered on the frontier like during the Civil War years.

In the words of historian Jeffry D. Wert who described her early managerial skills and talents during the Civil War years, which continued unabated in the postwar years for the Custer family: Eliza "soon began to rule headquarters as effectively and firmly as Custer commanded on the battlefield" in America's bloodiest war.[51]

Therefore, when Eliza journeyed west with Custer and Elizabeth, she had gone forth with lofty expectations held by the newly-appointed lieutenant colonel, who knew what she could accomplish from having seen her in action under wartime stresses and challenges at his mobile cavalry headquarters from 1863-1865. Therefore, like Elizabeth, Custer and Eliza, who were very much kindred spirits, opened up new chapters of their respective careers at Fort Riley, which was located in the Flint Hills region of northcentral Kansas.

Here, at Fort Riley, Eliza caught her first sight of the Buffalo Soldiers, the black soldiers, mostly former slaves like herself. These men of African heritage continued the noble traditions and distinguished service of the hard-fighting men of the USCT regiments during the Civil War. Six black regular regiments, four infantry and two cavalry, had been authorized by Congress in late July 1866 to meet the stiff demands of service in the postwar West and to guarantee that African Americans remained a permanent presence in the United States military establishment.[52]

Here, at Fort Riley, Eliza first saw the men of the 38th United States Infantry that had been created in the summer of 1866. This infantry command was one of the new Buffalo Soldier regiments which had been formed based on the excellent performance of black soldiers, who had served in the USCT units during the Civil War.

And, here at Fort Riley by the spring of 1867, Eliza perhaps saw a young African-American woman, even though she was not recognizable as a female in her loose-fitting blue uniform, in the regiment's ranks, because she was well-disguised as a male, Cathy Williams, or Private William Cathay.

Like Eliza, Cathy had been born as a slave, but on the other side of the Mississippi River in Missouri about the same period as herself in Virginia. And like Eliza, Cathy had first found a safe and secure refuge in the Union Army as a cook and laundress during the war years, after having escaped slavery forever in June 1861 and more than two years before Eliza.

As a cook and laundress like Eliza, Cathy served in Union armies, including in Eliza's home state of Virginia and during the Shenandoah Valley Campaign of 1864 like

Eliza and Custer, and on both sides of the Mississippi River in both the Western and Eastern Theaters. For Union officers, Cathy served as a cook and laundress even longer than Eliza and for almost the entire length of the Civil War.

After the Civil War, Cathy Williams desired to continue her service in America's military establishment, which had become her surrogate home, since she could hardly return to her former life and ex-owner's house at Jefferson City, Missouri, which was the state capital of this border state that had been divided by the war.

Therefore, disguised as a man which was relatively easy because Cathy was tall and slim, she enlisted in Company A, 38th United States Infantry on November 15, 1866 at Jefferson Barracks, Missouri. Like Eliza beginning in October 1866, Cathy was assigned to Fort Riley, where she arrived in the spring of 1867. Cathy took pride in her service of nearly two years in total with the Buffalo Soldiers across the West, including during a demanding Apache Campaign in the rugged New Mexico's mountains.

In her own words that revealed a good deal of pride that she possessed in herself and her service to her country, Cathy Williams emphasized how she was "A GOOD SOLDIER [who] was never put in the guard house, no bayonet was ever put to my back [and] I carried my musket and did guard and other duties while in the army" of a regular regiment.[53]

Besides the first post assignment of this young female Buffalo Soldier from Missouri, Fort Riley was also destined to become the home of one of the most famous Buffalo Soldier regiments, whose reputation was destined to far exceeded that of Cathy's 38th United States Infantry, the 10th Cavalry. During the spring and summer of 1867, the 9th and 10th Cavalry, which had been formed at Fort Leavenworth, Kansas, began to serve in the West to initiate more than two decades of distinguished service by these two mounted Buffalo Soldier regiments.

By early August 1867, Fort Riley became the home of the 10th Cavalry, which was a regiment of mostly former slaves and this reliable black regiment was known for its low desertion rates compared to white regiments, including Custer's own 7th Cavalry.

Colonel Benjamin Grierson, a tall, gangly Civil War cavalry hero and former music teacher from the West with a distinct talent for composing music and inspiring bluecoat troopers, black or white, had eagerly accepted command of the 10th Cavalry at a time when most other white officers took lower rank just to command white troops. Determined to create the best possible troopers partly because he appreciated the martial qualities and lofty fighting spirit of the black troopers, Grierson boldly promised his wife in a letter that "Colored troops will hold their place in the Army of the United States as long as the government lasts."[54]

Grierson was just the kind of open-minded and talented commander needed by a fledgling Buffalo Soldier regiment of hard-riding troopers in an ultra-conservative and traditional army that was still anti-black in its general sentiments.

He had led one of the audacious raids of the Civil War when his cavalry command of western horse soldiers slashed more than 600 miles through the Deep South and in Vicksburg's rear to astound a confused Rebel leadership during the late spring and early summer of 1863: a most effective cavalry diversion, while the relentless General Grant was making his skillful tactical moves with his western army that eventually resulted in Vicksburg's capture and the splitting of the Confederacy in two: a key turning point of the war.

Open-minded and free-thinking, Grierson believed completely in the qualities of his hardy fighting men of African descent and fought for them in the face of racists, including his own superiors, at great risk to his career and reputation. The Pennsylvania-born Grierson was determined that his black cavalrymen would receive fair and equal treatment and the same as white troopers wherever they served throughout the West.

Consequently, when the commander of Fort Leavenworth, Kansas, which was located around 20 miles northwest of Kansas City, Colonel William Hoffman, ordered that black troopers were not allowed to stand beside white troops on the fort's parade ground and to his credit, Grierson openly defied his superior's race-based directive. He then sent a written protest to department headquarters at the risk of a court martial and other troubles with the military establishment.

Most important, Grierson had boldly and early served notice to white leadership that the black horse-soldiers of the 10th Cavalry should be treated with fairness and equality, while protecting the dignity of the black regiment and its faithful members by taking determined stands against racism.[55]

Meanwhile, the western frontier and the central plains suddenly became even more dangerous for Eliza and other inhabitants of Fort Riley, isolated Kansas settlers and communities, and the scattered Buffalo Soldier detachments that had been assigned to guarding the Kansas Pacific

Railroad, whose iron tracks continued to be laid across the virgin prairies and toward the setting sun.

A military disaster struck rocked the western frontier. After the wiping out of Connecticut-born Captain William Judd Fetterman, a West Pointer and Civil War hero twice cited for gallantry, and his command of eighty cavalrymen in a resounding Sioux victory that was naturally declared by the press to have been a "Massacre" just outside the gates of Fort Phil Kearny, nestled among the picturesque countryside of northeast Wyoming, in December 1866, a forceful response from the United States Army became absolutely necessary.

Ironically, the gifted warrior Crazy Horse, a leading Sioux war chief who loved the land that he defended with his life, orchestrated the one-sided victory over the hapless Fetterman and he was destined to play a leading role in Custer's demise at the Little Bighorn.

In consequence, General Winfield Scott Hancock's punitive expedition, which included the novice Indian fighter Lieutenant Colonel Custer and the troopers of his inexperienced 7th Cavalry, was launched. This strike force, that never struck Native American war parties as optimistically envisioned at headquarters, was calculated to awe the hostile tribes into submission by its military might aligned and on the move on the open plains: an overly-optimistic and muddled concept that stemmed from hubris at headquarters.

However, to the white man's thinking across the West, the Fetterman "Massacre" called for vengeance, although it was a legitimate Sioux victory, like later at the Little Bighorn, based on brilliant tactics that even experienced West Pointers failed to understand or accept as legitimate: a guarantee that more young men and boys in blue uniforms would have to die in the future.

A hero of Gettysburg especially in helping to hurl back Pickett's Charge in the stubborn defense of Cemetery Ridge on the final day at Gettysburg, while Custer displayed his heroics on the East Cavalry Field in the rear of the Cemetery Ridge defensive line, Hancock was no Indian fighter like Custer. And his overly-ambitious spring 1867 campaign, with no clear objectives or targets because he faced ever-elusive warriors constantly on the move with stealth, was doomed to frustration and failure from the start.

The classic cases of Fetterman, Custer, and Hancock demonstrated the near-impossibility for Civil War heroes, who had won their glory in the art of conventional warfare only few years before, to successfully transfer their prior successes to the irregular war of Indian fighting: the toughest of all transitions, regardless of how successful a Civil War veteran had been from 1861-1865. Of course, this undeniable realty was a shocking wake-up call for Custer and others.

Ironically, Hancock's ill-fated expedition that foundered on the Great Plains only stirred up the Indians to new furies, fueling the Native American desire to take revenge on the whites, both soldiers in blue and civilians. Quite simply, Hancock's combined inexperience, arrogance, and over-confidence had proved to be a toxic blend that had only incited a full-scale Indian War on the central and southern plains.

Nothing had infuriated Native Americans more than Hancock's ill-advised decision to burn down Native American villages in an ugly taste of total warfare, which had been the formula for decisive success when taking the war to the Southern civilian population during the Civil War.

During "Hancock's War" that was denounced in the east by the press as having unnecessarily caused yet another costly and ill-fated Indian War, Custer met with bitter frustration in failing to come to grips with the Sioux during his pursuit of fast-moving war parties: a futility that was widely shared by even the finest veterans of the Civil War.

As he penned about the most frustrating of his campaigns because during the fruitless pursuit "neither myself nor any of the soldiers had caught sight of any Indians," who relied on hit-and-run tactics and staying out of harm's way. Wearing out their best horses and most experienced troopers in futile chases of an ever-elusive opponent, who seemingly always disappeared like ghosts over the grass-covered horizon which was so unlike the regular Confederate troops of Lee's Army, Custer failed to achieve the victory that had so eagerly anticipated and once considered inevitable.

For Custer, this conflict in the West was an entirely new kind of war, and unlike any kind of fighting he had previously experienced. Clearly, the former Civil War hero knew that he had a lot to learn about Indian warfare and the Great Plains. Custer's inability to learn invaluable lessons about the tactical nuances of Indian warfare and Native American psychology were destined to pave the way to disaster at the Little Bighorn.[56]

As noted, Custer now realized that he was in over his head in the strange and incomprehensible art of Indian fighting and his overall performance on the Great Plains was in fact "dismal." Confounded by an alien environment and resourceful enemy who refused to stand and fight like the finest rebel troops back in Virginia, a thoroughly befuddled

Custer faced a most vexing dilemma--the same kind that would again arise to doom him and five 7th Cavalry companies along the Little Bighorn–which he explained with surprise and amazement: "Alas for human calculations! The Indians, by means of the small reconnoitering parties . . . had kept themselves constantly informed regarding our movements and progress [and just] when it was finally clear to be seen that, in the race as it was then being run, the white man was sure to win, the proverbial cunning of the red man came to his rescue and thwarted the plans of his pursuers."[57]

Custer's list of failures in Hancock's ill-fated campaign left him reeling because of a number of startling new realities, shattering his illusions and confidence about not only his own military abilities, but also those of his troopers of the 7th Cavalry. Clearly, neither West Point nor the Civil War had adequately prepared Custer for the stern challenges that he now faced on the Great Plains.

Here, on the seemingly endless stretches of the open plains that resembled the vast sea in its sheer expansiveness and seemingly limitlessness, what happened on the East Cavalry Field and the glory that had been won by Custer on the afternoon of July 3, 1863 no longer mattered on the Great Plains.

Like Elizabeth who had long looked at her dashing husband as almost a God on the battlefield where his lengthy list of Civil War successes had come so often in the past, Eliza also had never seen Custer as a failure, which almost certainly came as a surprise, if not a shock, to her. Indeed, after scouring hundreds of miles during a four-month period during the course of Hancock's expedition, Custer had not only failed to achieve victory and win the glory that he had once anticipated, but he also had not even found any Native American warriors to fight in the ultimate humiliation.[58]

Quite suddenly, everything in the traditional art of warfighting from the heady days of the Civil War had dramatically changed for Custer in a new place and a new kind of conflict that he never fully understood or mastered as was revealed in full in the most tragic way at the Little Bighorn in less than a decade.

Part II
The Forgotten Secret Relationship

Chapter IV

Wartime Casual Sex and Custer

By any measure, one of the most famous Civil War photographs of the Custer family—the successful Union general, Elizabeth, and Eliza—might well be the most remarkable of Custer images, because of the forgotten story that it has told. If any Custer photo might be described as a picture worth a thousand words, then it was this wartime photograph taken by Matthew Brady not long before the end of the Civil War.

Therefore, as fate would have it, this well-known photograph is certainly the best one <u>not</u> of either Custer and Elizabeth, but of the forgotten Eliza. Consequently, Eliza's image from this famous photograph now graces the cover of this current book to reveal the real woman in her natural, typically modest, and homespun glory for the first time.

Most of all and as mentioned, this unique photograph—the only one that included Eliza--has been most revealing on a number of levels to tell a tale. First and foremost, this Civil War photograph has portrayed Elizabeth in all her pride and vanity that was excessive to say the least: dressed in her most expensive and finest riding outfit that she had purchased in the East, in excellent health and spirits, overjoyed in her husband's military successes, and looking proud and extremely vain, if not pompous.

Even more, it is obvious that Elizabeth was almost certainly the one person of this trio of subjects, who had most desired to have this photo taken in the first place. In striking contrast, Custer is looking his worst: haggard, tired, and thin from arduous campaigning in the field and especially from having recently led his cavalry to overcome challenges and win victories, while only on a brief leave to visit his wife.

Most revealing, he is looking away from the camera as if bored or perhaps even irritated to a degree, knowing that he was wasting away in cantering to his wife's whims, while seemingly lamenting the fact that he was now away for his hard-fighting troopers and the army that he loved, when he should still be leading the way on the battlefield.

Meanwhile, Elizbeth is looking straight at the camera during her proudest moment or so it seemed, while Custer appears entirely disinterested and caring little about what the cameraman desired or how he appeared for prosperity and much like Eliza, had also been suddenly removed from her duties to have this ill-timed photograph taken.

After all, Custer knew that he still had a hard and bloody war to fight to the bitter end, while Elizabeth was primarily focused on expensive buying sprees and city delights in the nation's capital not found in her native Monroe, when her husband was risking his life on one battlefield after another.

However, much like Custer, Eliza looks extremely bored in his photograph while she looks straight into the camera as if was her duty to fulfill the photograph's requests, after having been taken from her daily tasks to appear with her so-called "family," which was Custer's headquarters, Cavalry Corps, Army of the Potomac. She is wearing her striped bandana (it is not known but evidently the stripes are colorful, either red or blue) and plain calico dress with balloon sleeves and a large white scarf tied around her neck.

Like Custer, the modest-looking, plain, and humble-looking Eliza appears to be longing to be elsewhere and quite unlike Elizabeth, who is clearly basking in her considerable vanity and pride. Both Custer and Eliza look like they had been almost—which was very likely the case-- dragged into the photograph's studio in Washington, D.C., against their wishes and in obedience to Libbie's selfish desires, when they knew they should be elsewhere because duty still called. Indeed, at this time, Elizabeth was enjoying a vacation and life of luxury, while her husband risked his life on the battlefield. She might have just bought her fancy riding suit and simply desired to show it off before the camera, after another buying spree.

Sitting like Elizabeth while Custer is standing and appearing gaunt, Eliza looks stoic and calm—a classic portrait of simply dignity--while appearing at the camera without any expression on her face other than weariness and boredom at the entire proceedings, which were probably too long and problematic in conforming to the perfectionist photographer's dictates at the downtown studio in Washington, D.C.: the exact opposite of the appearance of a beaming Elizabeth and a seemingly distracted and equally bored Custer who mirrors Eliza's attitude of disinterest.

As mentioned, this famous Civil War photograph by Matthew Brady is certainly worth a thousand words, while revealing how Custer and Eliza often shared the same feelings and sentiments that ran contrary to those of the aristocratic blueblood Elizabeth, who delighted in personal pleasures sometimes at the expense of others like at this time. Today, one can only wish that Eliza had been in a good mood at this photographic studio, presenting a beaming smile at the time to reveal her natural beauty and spirit as known to Custer.

Unlike this most revealing photograph taken by Brady, the Custer myth and legend has not only long obscured the real Custer to millions of Americans for generations, but also has even obscured the people around him at the time.

Of course, the creation of the cavalier myth and glorification of Custer first reached unprecedented heights during the Civil War years, when the North needed a romantic hero to worship to inspire the northern populace and fuel the war effort during the dark days of 1864.

This situation was especially the case before Abraham Lincoln's all-important reelection in early November 1864, when the American people voted to persecute the war to the bitter end, thanks largely to recent Union victories like the fall of Atlanta, Georgia.

Then, after the Civil War and in much the same way, Custer then became a media creation of the eastern press and viewed by the public as America's premier Indian fighter, despite his inexperience, failures, and questionable actions on the Great Plains that indicated quite the opposite. In truth, Custer's much-touted and widely-publicized Indian-fighting skills, of course, would prove fatal to him and more than 200 of his more than 200 troopers of five 7th Cavalry companies at the Little Bighorn.

The mythical Custer, thanks to a favorable eastern press and his own self-promotional efforts that resulted in the continuance of his premier Indian fighter image an adoring public, was created for an extended period of more than a dozen years, before his tragic end came on June 25, 1876, when a brutal reality was revealed in full. In Custer's case, public perceptions and automatic assumptions without benefit of the hard facts, especially the belief that Custer was one of America's greatest Indian fighters, were more important than the reality, which finally caught up with Custer along the Little Bighorn.

Then, after his June 25, 1876 death and in promoting Custer's memory to counter all critics who blamed him for the Little Bighorn disaster, Libbie's trilogy of popular books fueled the rise of even greater romance and myth about the "flawless cavalier," who was portrayed as more saint than human being. This popular view of Custer in the eyes of a loving wife, who still grieved for her husband, became the standard view of the American people.

Elizabeth was destined to never remarry. She devoted the rest of her life—more than a half century until she finally died in 1933 during Adolf Hitler's rise in Nazi Germany—to the shameless promotion of Custer's pristine and glorified image for the public.[59]

In truth to this day after more than a century and a half, relatively little has been explored about Custer and his life beyond the myth and the romantic legend that had shrouded his image in an unrealistic light of excessive glorification and much like that of George Washington, who had likewise been placed atop an ivory tower by Americans since the American Revolution.

Despite the overabundance of Custer biographies and popularity of all things Custer to an admiring public, the most unexplored and forgotten aspect of Custer's life by far was his close relationship that he shared with Eliza Brown, especially of a sexual nature.

Quite simply, this intimate relationship with Eliza Denison Brown was Custer's greatest secret and has remained so until this day—more than 150 years later. Both during the Civil War and afterward, rumors swirled during the war years among his cavalrymen, both officers and enlisted men, that Custer was actively engaged in a sexual relationship with Eliza, which was shocking to white audiences for a host of reasons.

First and foremost, Eliza was coal-black in color, his cook and laundress, and a former slave who had attached herself to Custer's headquarters for years. Therefore, to whites of the day, such an intimate interracial relationship was not only unimaginable but also the worst of horrors, because Eliza was extremely black in color and, consequently, a sexual relationship was viewed as nothing less than a debauchery. Indeed, the news of such an interracial relationship would have stained the character, image, and morals of Custer like no other development, because of the traditional white perspective that was European-based and decidedly anti-black.

However, because Custer was so beloved and highly-revered by the Michigan troopers of his tough Wolverine brigade, Army of the Potomac, and since he possessed winning ways on the battlefield that began at Gettysburg on the decisive afternoon of July 3 to thrill the northern public, the secret about the true depth of the Custer-Eliza relationship was kept out of the newspapers and public eye out of necessity to keep the image of a sainted hero alive and well: a fact which ensured that this special relationship between a revered general and ex-slave was overlooked by Americans historians for generations and to this day.

In addition, Custer's early February 1864 marriage to Libbie likewise helped to mask the nature and depths of this secret relationship and helped to silence the swirl of rumors, which were part of the soldier grapevine, that included sexual activity.[60]

However, Custer never lost his pristine and glorified image, despite the rumors of the most recent of relationship with Eliza. Historians have long emphasized the famous "Custer's Luck" throughout his distinguished Civil War career and which was displayed on so many battlefields until it ran out along the Little Bighorn in the Montana Territory. But, ironically, they have never applied Custer's uncanny degree of luck and good fortune to this thorough silencing, where it truly belonged, which has long shrouded the fundamental truths about the Custer-Eliza relationship.

In regard to public image and as mentioned, Custer never lost his lofty standing partly because of the general silencing of this interracial relationship, which would have shocked the American public almost as much as his death at the Little Bighorn. Although he lost some respect in the eyes of most of his men in the Civil War and in the Indian Wars because of his favoritism that he so often openly demonstrated toward Eliza for an extended period, it failed to translate into public exposure or censure like in the case of the Thomas Jefferson and Sally Hemings relationship in 1802.

The glorified image of the romantic Custer, the stainless, chivalric knight and dashing cavalier early developed and only continued to grow over the years—first in the 1860s and then past the mid-1870s--to reach such lofty proportions that they became mythical. The development of the Custer myth and romantic legend that supported the traditional Victorian value system of America's ruling class--which contrasted sharply with the reality--left no place for the glorified Custer story, which explained why bluecoat troopers early gave Eliza an unforgettable sobriquet because of her constant presence and the favoritism shown her by Custer at headquarters.

It was common knowledge that a sexual relationship existed between the dashing general and former slave to provide the most forgotten explanation for a single female, especially an attractive one, having been a permanent presence at a commander's headquarters for an extended period, including even after the war when Custer now longer possessed a staff, while becoming known as "the Queen of Sheba."

Some of these bluecoat troopers, including the Michigan Wolverines who were Custer's favorites of his crack cavalry brigade and then division, Army of the Potomac, had seen the close personal interaction between the two in camp, perhaps even intimacy or evidence of it, and an unprecedented degree of affection that existed between their commander and Eliza.[61]

A high-ranking leader, especially a married one after February 1864, having an attractive young female at his headquarters for physical comfort and sex was not an uncommon sight during the Civil War. In fact, such military mistresses were common knowledge and widely-accepted as just part of military life that extended back centuries. Indeed, this distinctive perk or privilege of military men in high command faithfully continued a sexual legacy extending back to the beginning of the history of warfare.

Long had European Armies, especially those of Napoleon who Custer had studied in detail at West Point, been described in the nineteenth century as little more than "travelling brothels," in the words of a French officer of one of Napoleon Bonaparte's armies in Spain. However, because this was a religious age in the United States and American sexual values were more strict in the 1860s than in Europe during the Napoleonic Era, Civil War officers were much less guilty of this common practice of having a sexy companion, even when the esteemed general was married, than Napoleonic leaders earlier in the nineteenth century.[62]

First and foremost and reflecting his times, Custer was no saint as revealed in his own writings and those of his wife, and this fact included matters of sex.[63] A good many of his men, especially those of Custer's Michigan brigade who were around him and his headquarters most frequently during the Civil War years, "were aware of many of his derelictions," in the words of Captain Frederick William Benteen, who had served in a Missouri Union Cavalry regiment in the Civil War and then in Custer's own 7th Cavalry, in regard to sex outside marriage to Libbie.[64]

And in Custer's own letters to his wife, he was surprisingly open about sex, referring to his penis as "our mutual friend." According to the ardent Custer, only Libbie's presence in camp could cure "the want and cravings of 'our mutual friend'."[65]

But was this revealing sexual declaration by Custer also the case before his marriage, when he was in need of sexual contact and physical relief? Clearly, by way of his own words, Custer was a healthy young male with an active libido and active curiosity about sex, including when it came to attractive female members of other races. If Custer's words about his sexual longings referred to Elizabeth after his marriage, then what about the period before his early February 1864 marriage? After all, a more than six-month period existed when attractive Eliza was nearby and readily available and willing in camp at a time when Custer was in need of a sexual partner.

If Custer, a middle class product from rural Ohio and a young man who had not been raised around blacks because Ohio was a free state, made such sexual references to his upper-class wife of fine education and high social standing, then his behavior and verbiage, including sexual, in a military camp were certainly rougher and more extreme, especially if an young, attractive black woman was set-up in his presence at headquarters for an extended period and available for his pleasure like Eliza.

This undeniable fact of such common situations in which a military man with power, privilege, and means took advantage of sexual opportunities and engaged in sexual escapades when far from home, family, and social norms should not be surprising in a wartime environment, especially when an officer might not live to see the next sunrise, as Custer fully realized.

In fact, the sport of whoring by military leaders in the encampment and headquarters was only part of the overall military experience, and the Civil War was no exception to the rule. As since time immemorial when humans first waged war far from home, soldiers took sex where they found it without romantic illusions and societal sensibilities, while seldom asking questions in regard to notions about improper behavior that had existed in civilian society before the war.

However, all evidence has supported the view that Custer was not guilty of any kind of sexual abuse in his personal relationship with Eliza or any other woman for that matter, and any sexual activity between the general and former slave was distinguished by mutual consent, especially before his marriage to Libbie, as indicated from all existing evidence. After all, Custer and Eliza were two attractive individuals who were young, active, and full of life, while sharing the same dangers and hardships when on campaign together across Virginia.

In this regard and despite all of the books that have romanticized Custer's life and championed his chivalric virtues, especially the popular works penned by Libbie who was determined to keep the mythical Custer and his romantic legend alive and well long after his death, Custer was no different in regard to military men who have long engaged in casual sexual relations, because a lust fueled by the stresses of the conflict and wartime environment, when free sex was the norm, including in modern times.

However, generations of historians and writers have long drawn a perfect romanticized and Victorian Era veil over Custer's private and sexual life, especially outside of his marriage to protect the sensibilities and lofty Victorian image manufactured by Libbie, because of hero worship and the power of the enduring Custer legend and myth that have long obscured the most private aspects about Custer's life.

Of the hundreds of books devoted to the Custer story and especially those works that have focused on Elizabeth, no historian has previously explored the forgotten secret sex life of George Armstrong Custer when it came to the obscure subject of so-called camp followers, especially in Eliza's case, except this author.

First and foremost, Custer was a soldier with the same vices and virtues of other fighting men, regardless of culture, time, race, or what nation or cause for which they fought during wartime primarily because a professional soldier, including generals, never knew if he would see the next sunrise: a stressful and pressure-packed situation that called for a close embrace of the realistic philosophy of only living for the moment, because the next day might well be the last one for them.

Custer was certainly not immune to this longtime common fighting man concept of living only for the moment or day in the midst of wartime, especially because he was a notorious risk-taker on the battlefield, including in leading headlong cavalry charges like twice on the East Cavalry Field at Gettysburg, when Custer and his hard-fighting Wolverines had saved the day in the Army of the Potomac's rear on July 3.

A soldier having sex for sex's sake on a casual basis and with a newly-met partner was simply part of the most human and normal of all wartime experiences in a risky environment that held no promises or guarantees, despite the fact that the Civil War has been long viewed and portrayed by generations of historians and the veterans themselves, who wrote their memoirs about a conflict in which sex was absent and unimportant in the prevalent societal and Victorian Era traditions of the day.

Interestingly, if sex was mentioned by a Union soldier at all in a letter to a male friend rather than family, it was usually only in regard to sex with slave women and usually of a nonconsensual basis. To the average Civil War soldier, both Union and Confederate, a female slave or a newly-freed black woman were considered fair game in the sexual arena.

During the Civil War period and for long afterward, sex has been simply a taboo subject in America, especially to historians, which revealed the legacies of the nation's early strict Puritan roots of the seventeenth century and an excessive morality that was almost monk-like in many regards, especially when it came to sex.

But contrary to popular stereotypes and like any other wartime periods throughout the course of history, the Civil War period was actually a highly sexually-charged age. Many Civil War soldiers on both sides took advantage of easy sex wherever and whenever they found it, and the easier and more casual kind was found with slave women and especially contraband women who were without permanent homes, after having escaped slavery and remained vulnerable when in Union camps filled with young men who had not been with wives or girlfriends for lengthy period of time.

In Washington, D.C., President Abraham Lincoln often openly told jokes about sex in the White House to the shock of refined, upper-class easterners, who were not familiar with rougher and more open brand of typical western frontier humor that included sexual activity as a primary topic.[66]

Like so many other commanders who were not like the sexually-repressed Robert E. Lee, Stonewall Jackson, and other older generation of more traditional Civil War leaders who became the stereotypical "unstained, almost-celibate, and totally nonadulterous Civil War figures," and embraced the norms of human biology and physicality, Custer was the anthesis of this sexually-repressed stereotype of the Civil War leader. Custer defied the enduring myth of the spotless, pristine morality of military leaders on the tented field in a holy crusade of fighting to save the Union and destroy slavery.

Historians have too often confused the morality of the war to destroy slavery with mortality in sexual matters of Union soldiers, especially leaders, when the two could not have been more different during the years of conflict. Compared to Lee, a distinguished Mexican-American War veteran, and other sexually-repressed older and traditional types who deplored improper conduct, especially in regard to sexual matters, based on Southern cultural values, Custer was a healthy and vigorous younger man of a new generation and a free-thinking westerner.

Even more and as noted, he was also a free-thinker who was unbounded by the chains of bygone age tradition and strict orthodoxy. In this sense, Custer was unburdened with the old-fashioned values of the older generation about sex, especially before he was married.[67]

Not surprisingly, given his youthful energy, fun-loving nature, and zest for life, Custer was more sexually healthy and active as a young, dynamic officer of the Army of the Potomac compared to the older and traditional officers, whose views about sex were far more Puritanical and prudish. And in this regard, Custer early took full advantage of the perks of his elevated position in the army's ranks before he married Libbie, because afterward he attempted to be a good husband, or so it seemed, in his regard, according most existing evidence.

Sexy Anna E. Jones

Compared to armies throughout the course of history and before the arrival for former slaves who fled to Union ranks in droves across the South, the average Civil War encampment was noticeably devoid of females. Female camp followers, especially the wives of the common soldiers, had long been a regular feature of armies around the world, especially in Europe but also including for both sides during the American Revolution, because this was the traditional way of eighteenth century warfare. Civil War armies broke with this longtime tradition of camp followers as it had been known to their revolutionary forefathers, when independence had been won.

Throughout the eighteenth century, female camp followers in American and European Armies ensured that there was also plenty of sex, both casual and between wives and husbands. In the British Army of redcoats, officers sometimes took the liberty of eloping with the pretty wives of men in the enlisted ranks and taking off with their attractive prizes.

During the winter of 1862-1863 and more than six months before Eliza became a regular and permanent feature at Custer's headquarters and before he was married, Custer also welcomed an attractive young woman to his encampment at a time when white women in the encampment were a rarity.

She was named Anna E. Jones. Anna had been born in Cambridge, Massachusetts, in 1844.By his own admission, Custer set her up at his headquarters more than half a year before Eliza's arrival, and, here, the enchanting Anna "remained at [my personal] headquarters," wrote Custer.[68]

Anna was an orphan with a penchant and sexual appetite for Union officers, especially generals, which included Custer. This situation at his own headquarters has provided some evidence that has suggested that Custer might well have basically switched from Anna to Eliza in regard to a secret sexual relationship to not only escape mounting negative publicity, but also to ensure greater secrecy. Indeed, no woman ensured greater secrecy when in came to a secret relationship than a former slave woman and recently escaped without a past.

After all, Custer had to maintain the respect of his men—a moral soldiery--and this meant obscuring what existed between him and Anna as much as possible. Therefore, Custer possessed many reasons to dispense of Anna because of an increasingly complex situation that later did not exist for him with Eliza. By comparison, Eliza provided a much easy and less complicated solution to a host of existing problems and complications for Custer.

Custer had already gotten himself into hot water with the alluring Anna, who was nothing less than a sexpot who possessed immense potential to cause serious problems. Wise to the ways of the world, especially in the sexual arena, young Anna's ample charms were irresistible to a host of general officers, who found easy sex with Anna with no strings attached.

Clearly, Anna's popularity, which partly indicated the extent of her abundant skills in the bedroom, among Army of the Potomac generals spoke highly of her beauty and seductive ways of which Custer was not immune.

Anna's infamous legacy for loose and casual sex with Union officers of a high rank began after she departed her New England home and guardians, a strict minister and his wife, at age seventeen and headed for Washington, D.C., at the war's beginning. First befriending New York-born General John Ellis Wool, a Virginia Military Institute graduate and a War of 1812 and Mexican War veteran, she secured a pass from him to visit Union forces encamped in Baltimore, Maryland, located just northeast of the nation's capital.

At this time and out of necessity, Baltimore was an early Union-occupied city because of its extensive pro-secessionist sentiments of its citizens and officials, including the mayor. President Lincoln, therefore, had early ordered the occupation of Baltimore, because it early posed a strategic threat to the nation's capital only a relatively short distance away.

Early in the war after President Abraham Lincoln ordered Federal troops to occupy Baltimore, large numbers of Union troops manned the city's network of defenses, including soldiers stationed on Federal Hill that overlooked the placid waters of Baltimore's wide inner harbor that resembled a peaceful lake. In Anna's own words from a sworn statement, "I had no particular object or business in the Army, but I went out of curiosity. I spent some months in this way [and] In various camps, I was furnished by the commanding officer with a tent and sometimes occupied quarters with the officers."[69]

She then returned to the Washington, D.C. and the Northern Virginia area with a New York Volunteer Infantry Regiment, where she slept with numerous Federals officers, while acquiring a wide-ranging reputation. But ever-ambitious and opportunistic, Anna was on the look-out for higher-ranking officers to seduce.

Aiming high, she then took up with dark-haired, handsome General Franz Sigel, born in the Grand Duchy of Baden in 1824, at his own personal headquarters at Fairfax Court House, Virginia. Sigel was an academy graduate in Germany and a veteran of the 1848 liberal revolution. He had migrated to the United States in the spring of 1852.

He was also a hero of the bitter war in Missouri, where Missouri Rebels, under General Sterling Price, had been defeated in the spring and summer of 1861 and this crucial border state was won for the Union by 1862. Sigel was also a married man, but this fact made no difference to seemingly everyone under the stress and pressure of a wartime environment. He had wed German immigrant Elsie Dulon in January 1854 which he described as "the happiest time" of his life, and then fathered three children.

A lover of liberty who had early rallied liberal Germans in St. Louis, Missouri, during 1861 to fight for the Union and played key roles in the battles that won Missouri before he transferred to the Eastern Theater, Sigel was a war hero who loved his wife and children. However, the handsome general was also a man with physical needs when under the pressure and stress of a wartime environment.

Indeed, Anna's testimony in her sworn statements have been proven true. General Sigel had occupied Fairfax Court House, Northern Virginia, in September 1862. In mid-September, Sigel's Corps of mostly Germans had been redesignated the Eleventh Corps, Army of the Potomac. Sigel's Corps consisted of three divisions, and he affectionately called his unit "the German Command" with a great deal of pride and affection. Fairfax Court House served not only as an advanced observation point, but also as Sigel's headquarters, where Anna stayed with her German general, who embraced European military traditions, from St. Louis.[70]

Then, after Sigel, who had graduated from a German military academy, and according to her sworn statement,

Anna took up with General Julius Stahl, a Hungarian of promise.[71] Once again, Anna's sworn statement rang true partly because General Stahl was one of Sigel's division commanders.[72]

From all appearances, Anna was a lustful, hot commodity that was passed around for the mutual enjoyment of the general officers. Evidently, she was pushed along by more prudent officers after they had physically satisfied themselves and in a timely manner before a scandal broke out and because she herself tired of the affair and needed new conquests to satisfy an insatiable sexual appetite.

Therefore, the ambitious Anna then moved on to more fertile ground and a greater challenge by targeting another general, after she had conquered another one of Lincoln's generals with her ample charms and seductive ways. Either way, this young, but experienced, adulteress knew had to maneuver within the military system with consummate skill, both in and out of bed, among the generals of the Army of the Potomac.[73]

Anna's immoral life as a paramour, or whore, to Union general officers continued unabated when she next linked up with New Jersey-born General Hugh Judson Kilpatrick. This hard-charging cavalry leader of the Army of the Potomac was a fellow West Pointer of the Class of 1861 like Custer.

Kilpatrick was reckless and impulsive, which made him a hard-hitting cavalry commander on the battlefield and a perfect target for Anna.

During this bloody war to save the Union and in time, Kilpatrick had his attractive female lovers dressed in disguise as men on his staff and they became permanent figures around his bedroom and headquarters. He even allowed one women to ride in a closed carriage—like Custer allowed Eliza which contributed to the "Queen of Sheba" reputation and camp gossip among this troopers--amid Kilpatrick's headquarters train, when on campaign at the head of his cavalry.

In these ways, Kilpatrick made sure that he had ready and easy sex available to him for extended periods, especially in 1864-1865. In addition, Kilpatrick did not discriminate when it came to women of color in the true dashing cavalier tradition.

Consequently, like a bold cavalier, he took a mulatto, or "yellow women" of mixed-blood unlike Eliza, named Molly to be his mistress for an extended period at least until she became pregnant with the general's child. Because Molly was "in the family way" and as noted, Kilpatrick then next relied on utilizing the strategy of women dressed as soldiers, which then became his most successful strategy and trademark in regard to his keeping of camp mistresses.

Because of her physical condition, the unfortunate Molly was reduced to washing the clothing of Kilpatrick's lovers in the ultimate humiliation. Kilpatrick's cavalrymen spread well-founded rumors about what they had seen and knew to be true about their commander's sexual antics. Therefore, Kilpatrick's sexual escapades were well known throughout the Union cavalry arm.

Promising cavalry leaders, like Custer and Kilpatrick, were the youngest and most dashing commanders in the Army of the Potomac, and taking risks, both on and off the battlefield and including in the bedroom, were simply another part (the most forgotten part) of the daring cavalrymen's mystique.

Because Molly was related to another black woman, Mrs. James Dick, General Kilpatrick shortly "now was trying to go back on her, but [Molly was determined that she] should stick to him and make him take care of the baby, for it was his."[74]

But before this parade of women of loose morals and outrageously crafty utilizers of their raw sexuality and feminine wiles to advance themselves, there was Anna E. Jones, and General Kilpatrick became her next lover. Anna once again lay in bed with another Union general to engage in what she did best. However, after conquering Kilpatrick, she also was still unsatisfied and yet unfulfilled as usual because the real thrill for her was in the chase and the game of love and sex. She, therefore, was early ready to move on from Kilpatrick like so often in the past.

The dashing, handsome Custer naturally caught her ever-wandering eye, and vice versa. Clearly, an impressed Custer saw Kilpatrick's scandalous behavior and learned from it because they were fellow West Pointers of the same class and two of the most aggressive commanders of the Army of the Potomac with reputations on the rise.

Following her typical pattern and in March 1862, Anna predictably then soon moved on. This time she took up with Custer before Eliza came into his life in late July 1863. Like other generals of the Army of the Potomac, he could not resist her beauty and ample charms that had already conquered one Union general after another with remarkable ease.

Strikingly beautiful and a master at the art of carnal pleasure while still only a teenager, Anna was almost too good to be true and Custer could not resist the easy opportunity. Almost certainly and although direct evidence has been lacking, a general's grapevine had quite likely helped to prepare the way for the Custer in terms of paving the way for the Anna E. Jones relationship, as the general very likely already knew what to expect when he bedded the young "sex kitten."

Therefore, Anna E. Jones soon engaged in a sexual relationship with Custer in the encampment before his appointment to brigadier general and before the arrival of Eliza. Not long afterward and in her own words from a sworn statement, the brazen Anna then "went to the front as a friend and companion of General Custer."[75] In this case, of course, the words "friend" and "companion" were the day's popular euphemisms for lover.

With his pride and vanity, which were considerable, bruised, General Kilpatrick regretted losing such a lovely prize and evidently an exquisite love-maker of the first degree. In a fit of rage, he charged Anna with the lie of having been a Confederate spy even though she was from Massachusetts and spoke with a distinct New England accent. But, of course and in truth, Anna was a lover of Yankee generals and not Rebels.[76]

Nevertheless, despite obviously issued out of spite and a mean spiritedness, Kilpatrick's outrageous charges were taken seriously at Union headquarters in a typically bureaucratic military establishment in which regulations and rules were too often more important than facts. Lieutenant Charles Shepard was assigned to investigate this sensitive matter and he completed a detailed report dated February 2, 1863. Of course, Kilpatrick's ego-driven charges against Anna and even an earlier charge against a jealous female rival, who also possessed ample charms, having been a Rebel spy were "baseless."[77]

Caught up in the controversary, Custer became involved in the official investigation because Anna had given a sworn statement under a solemn oath that was part of official army channels. Therefore, in March 1864 and two years after they had first met and he had enjoyed his own intimate affair with her and the month after he was married, Custer was forced to make an official rebuttal to Anna's charges of an improper relationship and ungentlemanly conduct.

Now a married man—since early February 1864--unlike when he had earlier had his relatively brief affair with the curvaceous Anna who had become a general target of general officer lusts, Custer offered the lamest of excuses that was almost laughable because of the extent of Anna's infamous past of successfully bedding one Union general after another with a finesse worthy of a beautiful, but psychopathic and neurotic, manipulator with the most seductive of ways.

A naive, non-legalistic-minded Custer from rural Ohio should have obtained legal advice from an experienced military lawyer, but he failed to do so for whatever reason perhaps the subject was simply too embarrassing: an example of Custer's poor judgement like in first saddling himself with the infamous Anna, who was a loud-mouth trouble-maker with the potential to destroy a West Pointer's career on a whim.

Attempting to paint a fanciful picture of the man-hungry Anna—Union generals who could only fill her considerable sexual appetite and youthful ego--as a high-minded Florence Nightingale or Clara Barton, who eventually founded the American Red Cross, he implicated himself by writing how Anne E. Jones "remained at my headquarters until she could ascertain whether her services were required at any of the hospitals . . . ."[78]

Just in case the Massachusetts-born Clara Barton, who established a well-deserved reputation as the "Angel of the Battlefield," excuse failed to prove his innocence, Custer desperately sought another angle in his attempt to cover the tracks of his past intimate relationship with Anna and erase a most embarrassing sexual past while serving his country, especially now that he was a married man.

After he had dutifully sent her away because of an official army order that forbid women from accompanying the army that eventually paved the way of Eliza's role since she was officially considered "contraband," the persistent Anna once again suddenly appeared in camp "under an escort furnished by Major General [Gouverneur K.] Warren," a West Pointer and one of the Army of the Potomac's top engineers, to see Custer three weeks later, according to his explanation.

Attempting the ploy of lamely explaining why Anna had been repeatedly appearing at his headquarters as if she was nothing more than a strange, curious random female and playing the patriotic angle to disguise any hint of improper or immoral conduct, Custer simply lied to clear his name. He explained that Anna had only wanted to see the front lines, because "Her whole object and purpose in being with the army seemed to be to distinguish herself by some deed of daring."[79]

Then, Custer played his ace in the hole (that his one-time love object was crazy), just in case his Clara Barton-like and patriot female warrior angles failed to clear his name and get him out of hot water. He simply wrote "in this respect alone [she desired to distinguish herself and] she seemed to be insane."[80]

In conclusion and desperate to silence the swirl of rumors of what was potentially a brewing scandal from spreading and perhaps even getting back to his new wife not long after his marriage, Custer saved his biggest lie for the last which defied a long list of undisputable facts. Hoping to escape a scandal that Libbie might hear about if it festered much longer to perhaps effectively shorten his rise on the fast track to higher promotion, he emphasized that "Her claim of intimacy with me and General Kilpatrick is simply untrue."[81]

After a careful survey of the historical record and Anna's sworn testimony and all existing evidence, historian Thomas P. Lowry, a military veteran and a physician, concluded with some amazement, if not astonishment, in regard to Anna E. Jones' remarkable sexual abilities and skills in the art of seduction of Mr. Lincoln's high-ranking officers, especially generals: "Here is a woman, in actual fact still a girl, who managed to involve herself with six generals, not to mention the less ranks and various civilian functionaries, many of whom [including Custer] were hard to put to defend themselves or had their careers ruined."[82]

Chapter V

The Most Forgotten Sexual Dynamics

Other than the myth that the Civil War was largely a sexless one in relative terms, because its participants, both blue and gray, were barely interested in or not engaging in any sex because of their strict values, religious ways, and high moral conduct, the war's other major myth–perhaps the greatest of all–was that white soldiers, especially those of the Union, had no interest in black women as sexual conquests in anyway shape or form. Of course, this myth has been based of a combination of white racism, prejudice, and European-based standards of beauty.

However, in fact and demonstrated by the extensive record of racial intermixing throughout the course of history from the first contacts between black and white in early America, nothing could have been farther from the truth, because this has been nothing more than a traditional white perspective of what had been deemed as proper conduct of a sexual nature within strict racial boundaries.[83]

Indeed, in a groundbreaking study of sexual dynamics in the Civil War, Thomas P. Lowry made one of quite a few on-target revelations about soldiers of the Civil War that had been long absent from the history books, especially in the biographies of famous Union generals, including books about Custer. Indeed, nothing more surprised Lowry during his extensive research over the years than the remarkable fact that the "Yankee soldiers were happy to see white women, but they seemed fascination by black women."[84] Most important, this analysis was no exaggeration or hyperbole.

And Custer was no exception to this fundamental rule and basic fact of life in regard to healthy white males in blue uniforms when it came to sexually exploiting black women, both slave and recently freed during the war years. Significantly, few, if any white historians, over the years have revealed this undeniable truth about the war's most forgotten and overlooked sexual dynamics (interracial) that has been fully verified by the facts found in the historical record, despite such a wartime phenomenon having long seemed incomprehensible to so many white historians.

As Eliza described the initial mutual attraction, if only purely physical at first, felt by herself and Custer, upon their first meeting at the contraband camp of escaped slaves at his cavalry encampment at Amissville, Virginia, in late July 1863, when Custer and a captain on his staff suddenly "cum up to me, and the Ginnel says, 'Well, what's *your* name! I told him Eliza; and he says, looking me all over fust, 'Well, Eliza, would you like to cum and live with me?' I waited a minute [and] I looked *him* all over, too, and finally I sez, 'I reckon I would' [and] So the bargain was fixed up."[85]

Clearly, Custer was attracted to Eliza for a variety of reasons, including because of her slim athletic build and exotic beauty distinguished by classic African features that possessed a unique physical appeal to him—truly forgotten fruit of an exotic nature for a young and relatively sexually inexperienced man from rural Ohio.

Indeed, "even as a lad, [Custer preferred and] liked women who were slenderly formed," as Libbie Custer learned to her frustration, because she enjoyed living the high life and, in consequence, gained weight over time unlike Eliza, especially when older. Indeed, despite an overall stout but muscular build that was stealth-like, Eliza still presented an overall slim appearance year after year.[86]

In fact and even while Libbie was young and considered a great beauty among whites, especially to the throng of ardent pursuers in her hometown of Monroe, Michigan, where she had been the most sought-after woman and greatest prize of seemingly all the community's young men, Custer "loved to torment me, by pointing out to what awful [large] proportions a woman weighing what was to me a requisite number of pounds sometimes arrived in old age."[87]

Only several years later after the first meeting between her and Custer at the Amissville, Virginia, contraband camp, Eliza had not lost any of her natural charms, considerable appeal, or her ways with men, regardless of color, including manipulating them in emotional ways during the complex game of love in which she often emerged as the winner.

For instance, an amazed Libbie, when stationed at Fort Riley, Kansas, described how, "There was one person who profited by the presence of the negro troops [or Buffalo Soldiers]. Our Eliza was such a belle, that she would have elevated them into too exalted a sphere to wait on us, had she not been accustomed to constant adulation from the officers' body-servants from the time, as she expressed it, when she 'entered the service.' Still, it was a distraction, of which she availed herself in our new post, to receive new beaux, tire to them, quarrel and discard them for fresh victims [and] They awaited on her assiduously [at least] as long brief season of favor lasted. They even sought to curry favor with Eliza by gifts to me."[88]

It is not known but perhaps at this point, Elizabeth might have looked at Eliza differently and with a somewhat more wary eye in regard to her close dealings and interactions with her husband, because she now saw the sexual power that Eliza easily held over men.

Indeed and most important, Eliza's sexual appeal was hardly limited to black soldiers, as Custer discovered himself from the first time that he had seen the alluring young black woman, who was alone, vulnerable, and needing a white male protector just after she had escaped slavery. In this regard, Custer truly played the role of the shining knight in armor for Eliza.[89]

Here, near the little town of Amissville amid the green, rolling hills of the Virginia Piedmont on a hot summer day, Eliza's strong physical appeal and overall attractive appearance resulted in the true beginning of the forgotten secret intimate relationship between Custer and Eliza that almost certainly lasted for months, before he marred Elizabeth in early February 1864.

Of course, Thomas Jefferson's and Sally Hemings' long-term sexual and all but guaranteed loving relationship has provided the best-known example of the power of the natural attraction that sometimes existed between whites of high status and slave women that had long thrived in Virginia since colonial days.

Some historians have speculated that some slave women, perhaps Hemings herself, encouraged and even initiated such sexual relationships with white masters for the future welfare of their resulting children in a racist society. Most historians have now concluded that this secret relationship in the privacy and seclusion of Monticello was based upon a long-existing affection, which resulted in a brood of children, such as Eston Hemings Jefferson, who were raised on the Virginia mountaintop in the Piedmont.[90]

Not unlike the irresistible Anna E. Jones, young and sexy to an inordinate degree, except for differences in color, Eliza was certainly not a beauty in the traditional sense, but she was certainly attractive and pretty in a natural way, which caught Custer's attention and prompted him to have first approached her to solicit her longtime presence at his headquarters. Of course, she readily accepted the unbelievable offer and Eliza's destiny thereafter was linked to Custer for more than half a decade.

More important, she was certainly alluring, sensual, and attractive enough that the members of Custer's Michigan brigade were convinced that a sexual relationship exited between Custer and Eliza, because they, no doubt, were a bit jealous and perhaps lusting themselves for this confident black woman, who had captivated Custer with her natural and instinctive ways. Ironically, unlike so many white historians to this day, Custer's men, who were his most faithful followers, fully accepted the view that a sexual relationship existed between the two and understood it unlike generations of modern historians.

After all, these were the same men who gave Eliza the most revealing nickname of "the Queen of Sheba," because of what they had repeatedly seen with their own eyes or heard from fellow comrades. However, her vibrant, fun-loving personality, and a rare measure of wisdom for one so young made Eliza even more appealing and attractive to Custer, proving that beauty existed inside this young former slave woman from the Virginia Piedmont.[91]

In a rare example of a white historian having acknowledged Eliza's special appeal of a pristine, natural attractiveness that was appreciated by Custer from the beginning, author Thomas A. Lewis correctly described her as Custer's "comely black cook named Eliza . . . ." [92] Most significant, this outright physical attraction that existed between Custer and Eliza was nothing less than a magnetic pull from the beginning, which certainly had something to do with the old proverb that "opposite attract."

Consequently, in the beginning and as mentioned, Custer had personally and carefully picked out the slender, young, and athletic Eliza out of a crowd of escaped Virginia slaves at the Amissville contraband encampment. With a physical yearning for sexual intercourse as he had previously demonstrated with sexy Anna E. Jones and almost certainly curious about the dynamics of interracial sex, which was something unknown and entirely new to him as a product from rural Ohio, to some degree, Custer personally selected Eliza in no small part because of her overall attractiveness, especially since his sudden offer to her to join his headquarters was of such an impetuous nature.

Most significant and revealing at the beginning, Custer had not initially asked Eliza if she could cook for him and his staff as generally assumed by historians, because this situation certainly seemed to have been the most natural development during their initial exchange of words in their first meeting based upon Custer's first sight of her at the contraband encampment of escaped slaves. Instead, the young brigadier general first said nothing about duties that she would have to perform at his headquarters, but Eliza had accepted the challenge without question.

In what Eliza described as a "bargain" in which she would be allowed to stay at his headquarters to be given food and shelter at a time when she had no means to provide for herself while on her own for the first time of her life, Custer had simply only asked her, "would you [come] and live with me?" Indeed and as noted, despite dressed as a typical female slave in a plain calico dress and wearing a bandana,

Eliza's overall attractiveness and West Indian-like female bearing of a natural grace, raw physicality, and subtle seductiveness had first caught Custer's eye, because he was a well-trained connoisseur of female beauty regardless of color or race, as revealed in his strong attraction for Indian women, especially Cheyenne, for which he later became far better known to historians.[93]

What cannot be denied was the fact that the combination of an ebony color, athletic build, and youthful attractiveness, including a natural sexuality that needed no kind of adornment or artificial enhancement, such as fashionable makeup or fancy eastern clothing like in Elizabeth's case, was certainly appealing to Custer.

As an enchanted and smitten, despite his marriage to Libbie and her traditional Anglo charms, Custer described one young Indian woman, the daughter of Chief Black Eagle of the Kiowa tribe, who caught his eye while serving on the Great Plains: "a young squaw, who certainly could not have reached the age which distinguishes the woman from the girl [who] was possessed of almost marvelous beauty, a beauty so remarkable . . . the most beautiful squaw [blessed with a] graceful and well-rounded form, her clearly-cut features, her dark expressive eyes, fringed with long silken lashes, cheeks rich with the color of youth, teeth of pearly whiteness . . . "[94]

In many ways and in appreciating a natural and pristine God-given feminine beauty in all varied forms, colors, and varieties, Custer might well have been describing Eliza, whose dark color, smooth skin, youthful attractiveness, shapely figure, upright carriage, fine facial features, graceful West Indian-like carriage and overall look, a nearly perfect set of white teeth, and large dark eyes that were cat-like equally drew Custer's attention at first sight.

However and partly because he was writing for a white audience and, of course, could not expound about aspects of a natural African female beauty because of the anti-black sentiments of the day, Custer reserved his most lavish praise for Native American female beauty. He especially emphasized the natural beauty of one Indian woman in particular, the daughter of Chief Little Rock of the Southern Cheyenne, Monahseetah.

Chief Little Rock had been born in the Black Hills around 1805 and led the Southern Cheyenne on the Washita River, when Custer struck with his 7th Cavalry in a surprise attack on the unprotected village, Oklahoma Territory, on November 27, 1868. Chief Little Rock was one of the many victims on that bloody day in which Custer and his 7th Cavalry first gained their Indian-fighting fame.

Using the same descriptive word of "comely" for Eliza employed by historian Thomas A. Lewis who was right on target in this regard, a smitten Custer described the young Southern Cheyenne woman named Monahseetah as "an exceedingly comely squaw, possessing a bright, cheery face, a countenance beaming with intelligence, and a disposition more included to be merry . . . She was probably under rather than over twenty years of age. Added to bright, laughing eyes, a set of pearly teeth, and a rich complexion, her well-shaped head was crowned with a luxuriant growth of the most beautiful silken tresses, rivalling [sic] in color the blackness of the raven and extending, when allowed to fall loosely over her shoulders, to below her waist. Her name was Monahseetah."[95]

Once again, Custer's description of Monahseetah could have applied to the equally young and attractive, both physically and in general manner that revealed a graceful dignity, Eliza, when Custer first approached her at the Amissville contraband camp and selected her for his cook and laundress from among a group of escaped slaves from the Virginia Piedmont.[96]

Most significant, generations of white historians have long been debated if Mo-nah-se-tah, or Monahseetah, bore Custer a child, after she was captured at the November 1868 massacre of Chief Little Rock's people by the 7th Cavalry at the Washita. After all, Custer had almost greedily kept the young beauty for himself thereafter.

White historians have mostly concluded that such a sexual relationship (like in regard to Eliza) was not the case largely because of their longtime hero worship of Custer. However, an abundant amount of Cheyenne oral history, which had now become more recognized by historians as accurate and worthy of note, has told a much different story: light-colored Yellow Bird, or Yellow Swallow, was in fact Custer's son of Monahseetah.

While the often-debated subject of Custer's paternity was less likely because he might have been sterile from venereal disease that he had gained in his West Point days, the likelihood that Custer had sex with Monahseetah was certainly much higher and almost a certainty.

For the rest of her life and for such reasons, she considered Custer her legitimate husband. Of course, Custer thought differently since he had no choice because he was already married and, of course, had to move on with his life, after having fulfilled his sexual passions with still another woman of color.

During his Civil War campaigns and like for Monahseetah in his Indian Campaigns on the Great Plains when he often wore his favorite buckskin coat which was a popular campaign garment among the 7th Cavalry's officers, Custer was unable to conceal his affection and admiration for Eliza. From the beginning and as noted, he bestowed a host of privileges that included a sizeable tent so Eliza that was so large that it doubled as a mess hall for his staff, and a "carriage," or buggy, which Custer described in a June 21, 1864 letter as "Eliza's carriage."[97]

All in all, this obvious favoritism lavished on Eliza from the beginning was rare and special treatment given to a former slave by the dotting Custer, because it was entirely unprecedented from any other Union general during the war years. In fact and as mentioned, Eliza had long received such special attention and treatment from Custer that she gained her common nickname among the troopers of the Michigan Brigade, "the Queen of Sheba."[98]

From having closely viewed the close interactions between Custer and Eliza over an extended period in close proximity at the headquarters camp where she remained a central and omnipresent figure, the Michigan Brigade's troopers had early concluded that their young, handsome commander and his young, attractive black cook were lovers, especially before Custer was married. Historian Lewis explained how their special relationship and bond "triggered persistent, dark rumors about his relationship with her . . ."[99]

However, Lewis, a white historian as noted, had no need to stain the idea of an intimate relationship by his emphasis that such rumors of sexual activity between Custer and his favorite black woman as "dark" because Eliza was blessed with traditional African physical and facial features of an attractive nature: in truth, there was nothing dark at all about a sexual relationship between the two based on mutual consent.

But this term of "dark" used by Mr. Lewis, a fine historian of talent, was a typical, almost subconscious, use of verbiage that has denoted a traditional degree of white negativity to an interracial relationship between two consenting adults (Custer and Eliza) and one marked by a good deal of mutual affection primarily because Eliza was black. However and to his credit Lewis correctly emphasized the extent of knowledge about the Custer-Eliza relationship that existed among the boys in blue throughout the Civil War years.

But, of course and as noted, the fact that a good deal of talk about their secret relationship were so-called "rumors" failed to mean that they were untrue, as in the case of the Custer—Monahseetah relationship that was certainly a real one. After all, rumors about the Jefferson-Sally Hemings relationship inside the insular world on the little mountaintop known as Monticello had long existed among the local people, including in Charlottesville, who knew the truth because it was common knowledge and nothing new. After all, generations of Virginia planters and female slaves had formed sexual relationships in this area for as long as anyone could remember. This kind of interracial activity was simply part of daily life in Virginia and across the South.

Jefferson's interracial activities at Monticello existed for nearly a decade, before they were finally exposed and became known to the American public at large by way of publication of the stunning story in a Richmond newspaper in September 1802 only because they were used as political ammunition against a sitting president.[100]

Historian Lewis was correct in describing what was indeed a *relationship* between Custer and Eliza and a special one that was common knowledge among the soldier grapevine that existed among the men of the Cavalry Corps of the Army of the Potomac like the civilian grapevine of Charlottesville in regard to the Jefferson-Hemings relationship: a fact that was partly evident in Custer's own words as written in letters in which he often mentioned Eliza and revealed that she was often on his mind to an ordinate degree. More important, Custer's words have also revealed the depth of his distinct affection and admiration for Eliza for an extended period of time, which consisted of more than half a decade and over the course of two wars.[101]

For such reasons in regard to the close relationship that existed between Custer and Eliza and although guilty of considerable understatement, historian Marguerite Merington, as if relying on a mature woman's well-honed intuition, discreetly concluded with accuracy how Eliza "became a figure of no minor importance in the Custer story."[102]

Getting right to the main point and to his credit, even an excellent Custer-admiring historian, Jeffry D. Wert, has at least recently acknowledged the special qualities of Custer's close "relationship with Eliza [which] has produced questions and controversy. He had affection for her, but did he share his bed with her?"[103]

As revealed by Wert, this was no idle speculation or meaningless gossip by the men of the Michigan Brigade about the depth of the Custer and Eliza relationship. Most important, they admired and loved Custer, and the fact that he had an intimate relationship with the "Queen of Sheba" did nothing to dim their faith in their aggressive, young commander, who always led the way to victory in dramatic fashion.

Therefore, when these cavalrymen openly talked about the "Queen of Sheba," these revelations were not meant to slander Custer's name or damage the young general's image. They were just commenting on a fact of life. Indeed, these soldiers, including the Michigan Wolverines, were merely stating facts as they knew them and referring to what had been seen at Custer's headquarters. [104]

As learned from a reliable source, Captain Frederick William Benteen, a man of courage both on and off the battlefield as a Union officer and later a leading officer of Custer's 7th Cavalry, openly explained what few others dared to mention at the time about one of America's great military heroes, because he was a dedicated Custer enemy. Like few others, he revealed the unvarnished truth as he knew it: "It was notorious" that Custer "used to sleep with his cook."[105]

Evidence has revealed that Custer's personal actions in camp were "notorious" because they involved sexual activity with Eliza. Besides Benteen, how many people knew of the depth of this secret relationship between Custer and Eliza? Of course and without any doubt, Elizabeth who was living with her family back in Monroe, Michigan, had no idea about what her husband have been doing in secret at the cavalry encampment of the Army of the Potomac in the past, including with Anna E. Jones before Eliza's arrival.

According to Captain Benteen, the fact that a sexual relationship existed between Custer and Eliza was common knowledge in the cavalry of the North's principal army in the eastern theater. As Captain Benteen wrote: "It was notorious throughout the Cav[alry] Corps [of the] Army of the Potomac that Gen. Custer used to sleep with his cook," Eliza Denison Brown, the former slave from the Virginia Piedmont.[106]

Emphasized to make Custer appear in the most negative terms in regard to lacking character and discretion, Benteen especially identified and emphasized the degree of Eliza's blackness–she was of pure African blood with no evidence of any past mixture with whites and clearly Benteen considered this racial factor as directly equating to the epitome of ugliness in keeping with the day's white standards of beauty--and prominent African facial features.

Clearly, Benteen specially emphasized this physical description as a means of demeaning Custer's taste in women. Displaying not only his book-learned education but also his ignorance and racism from a traditional Southern background, including his upbringing from a slave-owning family of Petersburg, Virginia, Benteen penned how Custer's "cook . . . was one of the blackest, most monkeyish looking African women ever turned out. (The Latin maxim *de gustibus non est disputandum* comes in here)–only it shows monstrous poor taste in the General; only a trifle of economy I suppose with him–and everyone who knew him, knew that he was penurious to the fullest extent of its meaning."[107]

In addition, Captain Benteen's use of the word "taste" was significant, because this fashionable term was a white and a Southern-based definition. Throughout the antebellum period of the 1850s, the word taste became the standard, operative term to denounce and discourage racial mixing, or amalgamation, that most biased Americans, both northerners and southerners, saw as nothing less than a betrayal of white racial values and traditions.

Therefore, as used by Benteen, the term taste appealed to the opinions of the American people in regard to the racial sin of interracial mixing because of their disenchantment with the abolitionist's efforts to bring full equality to blacks and to end slavery, since it fueled the all-consuming societal and cultural fear—very much of an obsession--that abolitionists possessed an aggressive pro-amalgamation agenda to transform American society.

However, the horror that nineteenth century whites felt toward the concept of racial intermixing was actually more theoretical than fact and most ironic, because such interracial activity had been as old as America's founding and as American as the proverbial apple pie.

Consequently, not only people of the South, but also most people of the North had long opposed the abolitionists, who were a small northern extremist fringe group throughout the 1850s, primarily because of the fear that they were bent on overturning the social order by promoting the sexual mixing of the races. White society's definition of proper moral behavior and the factor of taste have often served as an effective barrier not only to racial interaction and amalgamation, but also to any thought of bestowing equality to blacks, including free blacks in the North, or ending slavery in America before the Civil War.

In this sense to most Americans, slavery's horrors were much less terrifying than the alleged horrors of amalgamation, leading to the spread of ugly anti-abolitionist and anti-black riots in large cities across the North, including New York City, during the 1850s and then during the Civil War. Therefore, by employing the word taste and applying it to the Custer and Eliza relationship to reveal his Southern roots, Benteen was using a popular societal term of his time that had long bolstered the arguments of pro-slavery and anti-black equality sentiments of the American people in general.[108]

Clearly, in revealing his typical Southern attitude about blacks that extended back to his youth in Virginia at Petersburg, which was located just south of Richmond, and in keeping with white, or European, traditional and cultural standards of beauty, Benteen would have felt a less powerful sense of revulsion and disgust if Custer had enjoyed a relationship with a light-skinned, nearly white, and straight-haired Sally Heming-type. For ample good reason, Heming's striking beauty earned her the local nickname "Dashing Sally" among both whites and blacks.

Indeed, Sally's father was the highly-revered Dr. John Wayles, Jefferson's father-in-law and mentor whose legacy can partly be seen in the enlightened words of Jefferson's

Declaration of Independence, despite its heavy editing by Congressional members in early July 1776. Sally Hemings was the half-sister of Jefferson's first wife, Martha Skelton Wayles-Jefferson, who had left him a widower when relatively young.

Ironically, Captain Benteen almost certainly would not have condemned his fellow Virginian and Southerner, Jefferson who was known as the sage of Monticello, for what he so thoroughly denounced Custer and with such vehemence, because of Sally's whiteness compared to Eliza's traditional African features, darkness, and physicality.[109]

Since Benteen served in the western theater during the Civil War, he had learned the details and long-existing rumors–going back to 1863 before Custer's marriage to Elizabeth and which had existed among Custer's own Michigan men and other Federal soldiers, including the troopers who served in the Cavalry Corps, Army of the Potomac--about the Custer-Eliza relationship from an old friend.[110]

In a 1895 letter to D. F. Barry, Benteen explained how he had partly derived his information from the existing reliable common knowledge that he had "learned here [in Atlanta, Georgia, after he had retired from the United States Army in

July 1888] from an old Va. classmate" from the Petersburg Classical Institute, Petersburg, Virginia, where Benteen had received a fine education in the days of his youth.[111]

Ironically, this Virginia Confederate officer, especially if a cavalryman, might have learned as much if he had been captured by Custer's men who knew about the "Queen of Sheba," or had he captured some of Custer's troopers during the war years? Again reflecting his Southern background from a slave-owning family of Petersburg, Virginia, on the sluggish Appomattox River of a brownish hue, Benteen emphasized that Barry must certainly be "well, horrified" by the revelation about Custer's sexual appetite when it came to a former Virginia slave.[112]

In conclusion, Benteen explained to Barry that this information about the Custer-Eliza relationship "would't be thought of [as important] by the many knowing them [Custer and his wife], provided Mrs. Custer–who was aware of many of his derelictions in this regard, and others–did not attempt to throw such a gorgeous mantle of saintliness around him– and at the same time cause so much mud to be thrown on the character of his betters."[113]

However, generations of white historians, much like the legions of white Thomas Jefferson worshipers who have denied even the mere thought that he might have an intimate relationship with his slave Sally Hemings at Monticello for decades, have strongly denied any possibility of a Custer-Eliza relationship—the usual white response, especially from traditional and conservative historians--because such an interracial relationship (the ultimate horror to the vast majority of whites throughout the Victorian Era and throughout the Jim Crow era, when African Americans were economically, socially, and legally oppressed almost as much as in slavery by discriminatory national and state laws) would have sullied Custer's unblemished heroic image and romantic legacy, which has been glorified to no end for more than a century, in their minds.

As could be expected, the time-worn and extremely-flimsy central foundation of the lame anti-relationship argument was that Jefferson was far too principled and he was "morally above such behavior" when it came to a possible sexual relationship with a young slave woman, despite having been a normal, healthy man and widower and the fact that Sally Hemings was a rare beauty of exceptional overall quality: exactly the longtime excuse to defend other whites who had fostered children of enslaved black women, as seen in the case of the highly-respected Dr. Wayles, who was a leading pillar of his Virginia community and society.

Even after the 1998 DNA testing that sexually linked a "Jefferson" to the offspring of Sally Hemings which verified the rumors of their intimate relationship at Monticello as long charged, a new legion of critics emerged to proclaim that Thomas Jefferson was not the father. Instead, they then emphasized that it had been one of Jefferson's relatives who had been Sally's lover and not Thomas Jefferson, despite all of the collaborating evidence and black oral history, which had been long routinely dismissed as "fabrication" because of the color factor, that has indicated otherwise.

Therefore, in much the same way in the traditional white attitude and conclusion that was reminiscent of the longtime denial of the Jefferson-Hemings relationship, historian Jeffry D. Wert could only admit that Custer "had affection for her," but no more when he shied away from the most controversial subject of the Custer story like so many other historians.[114]

However, Custer's own words, which white historians have conveniently overlooked or ignored when it came to Eliza, have revealed the depth and extent of their mutual affection, including flirting and sexual inuendo, which has been long discounted by the large number of Custerphiles, although evidence has revealed otherwise and has existed for many years.

Quite simply and unfortunately, a subtle, almost unconscious racism, not even fully realized by these white historians who almost all male, traditional, and conservative generation after generation, especially in racial matters when it came to interracial sexual relationships, has played a part in overlooking this important relationship in Custer's life during the height of his fame and which began not long after his heroic performance in saving the day for the Union on the East Cavalry Field at Gettysburg.

Perhaps only a sensitive, intelligent woman could fully realize and understand the importance of the depths of this secret relationship on multiple levels, and gifted writer and historian Marguerite Merington first gave a measure of credence to the significance of the Custer-Eliza relationship.[115]

However, of course, in the years immediately following the Second World War's conclusion, when America was yet celebrating its success and that of its allies in having defeated the spread of fascism and glorifying its new heroes with nationalist pride, any mention of a possible relationship of a revered American hero with a black women of lowly antecedents was little more than sacrilegious and heresy.

And, at this time, this situation was especially the case when racial segregation was yet the law of the land because of Jim Crow's harsh dictates, which had been deeply-entrenched into state and national laws across America. Therefore, Marguerite Merington, a talented English-born (1857) American author, could not only make no mention of the intimate nature of the relationship, but only hint at it.

Since Custer's demise along the Little Big Horn on that awful June afternoon in the depths of the Montana Territory, American historians, who had long glorified and romanticized the Custer image like no other military figure n history, found no place for a young black woman whose acknowledgement by them on almost any level in connection to Custer, especially sexual, would have severely sullied the Custer mystique, especially in regard to his much romanticized relationship with Elizabeth.

As could be expected during an era of hero worship on an entirely uncritical level by historians and the American public in general because it was viewed as an essential part of patriotism, Benteen's words about the Custer-Eliza relationship have been casually dismissed by generations of historians also because he became a well-known enemy of Custer.

However, a sufficient amount of collaborating evidence has revealed the truth of Captain Benteen's well-founded charges, including that Custer's men called Eliza "the Queen of Sheba," because of the extremely-favorable treatment that she received from her Custer in an unprecedented fashion.

As mentioned, pro-Custer historians have long simply dismissed Benteen's words as those of an angry, bitter man, who was not to be believed on any level. However, this kind of casual dismissal was exactly the same response to those individuals (truth-tellers in this case), who had earlier emphasized that Jefferson had a longtime sexual relationship with his female slave, Sally Hemings, at Monticello.

Like almost all other traditional white writers and historians for generations, one historian, Jules C. Ladenheim, who wrote Benteen's biography with the biased-laden name of *Custer's Thorn*, has simply casually brushed aside Benteen's charges by writing how "Benteen relates that Custer had sex with his black female cook, which, according to Benteen, he had also done during the late war [which was the Civil War, but] The charge is most unfair."[116] However, in truth and as seen by this example that was typical, the automatic dismissal of Benteen's charges without serious investigation has been what was the most unfair over the years.

This traditional white historian and so many others like him, who had embraced the Custer romance of the glorified and saintly image, were correct at least in the sense that

Benteen's charges were certainly mean-spirited and meant to disparage Custer and blacken his character. However, they were guilty of omitting any possibility of a close relationship based upon not only mutual consent but also a measure of affection, if not love—a casual wartime level--to some degree. The most unvarnished truths in life have always hurt, and Benteen's words were no exception in this regard.

Worst of all and entirely unfair, what Benteen implied in his accusation was that Custer took advantage of a slave women in the typical Southern master exploitation tradition by way of coercion, aggressiveness, or even an act of rape because of his high rank and advantageous situation, which was certainly not the case as revealed by all available evidence. This was Benteen's most malicious attempt to damage Custer's reputation.

Indeed, if this had been the true situation, then Benteen would have succeeded in presenting the worst of all images of Custer as a sexual exploiter or perhaps even a rapist: obvious fabrications and untruths that were calculated to smear Custer's name.

However, like Jefferson in regard to his long-term relationship with Sally Hemings at Monticello, nothing about Custer's character or personality has indicated such possibilities that would have been horrific and tragic on multiple levels. After all, if Custer had forced himself on Eliza in an immoral manner, then he would have been no different from the many Southern plantation owners, who had long abused slave women and who he personally detested: a situation that he hated and called "evil."

It is not known but was Benteen, who was a white Southerner who had been around Virginia slaves, including attractive black females, and had known about this tragic aspect of the Southern experience all his life until the Civil War, when he broke with his family to side with the Union and join the boys in blue, actually providing some hints about his own sexual activities in pre-Civil War Petersburg, where he had been raised?[117]

In contrast to Benteen, Custer was a northerner from a small town in rural Ohio. From the beginning, therefore, he possessed much different views about slavery and slave women in general than Benteen, who hailed from one of Virginia's largest cities, and generations of other Southerners: in fact, they were very nearly the antithesis.

However and as noted, Custer's own words from his letters to his wife have revealed the deep affection–not lust that might have resulted in some kind of sexual abuse as hinted at by Benteen–and admiration that he possessed for Eliza in almost every way that even transcended some of

Libbie's personal qualities, which had been corrupted to a degree by her upper-class upbringing, elitist tastes, and sentiments.

One of Eliza's most admirable traits included bravery that had been repeatedly demonstrated by her before the enemy in the war zone, when Custer and Eliza shared the same dangers while campaigning in Virginia unlike Elizabeth, who was safely out of harm's way like a good white wife and as Custer desired, because he loved his wife.[118]

A close reading of Benteen's words from 1895–nearly two decades after Custer's death with more than 200 of his 7th Cavalry troopers at the Little Bighorn–revealed that he mentioned the Custer-Eliza relationship partly because both he and Illinois-born Marcus Albert Reno, Custer's other top lieutenant on June 25 1876, had become the scapegoats for having not come to their commander's assistance on June 25, 1876 to ensure Custer's defeat along the Little Bighorn and because Libbie and others in their writings about Custer continued to "attempt to throw such a gorgeous mantle of saintliness around him–and at the same time cause so much mud to be thrown on the character of his betters."[119]

Therefore, the primary argument of generations of historians against the fundamental truths of Benteen's 1895 words has been his intense personal hatred for Custer that lingered for decades, when in fact Benteen only mentioned the Custer-Eliza relationship privately in a letter to a friend long after his death and not in his writings or in an official statement to smear Custer's character: a fact that has been conveniently overlooked and ignored by historians, who have long worshipped at the altar of the Custer romance and glorification.

As mentioned, Benteen was only writing to a fellow Virginian and friend, D. F. Barry, about facts that were well known–which corresponded with Eliza's popular sobriquet of "the Queen of Sheba" that was well-known among the men of his Michigan brigade and other cavalry commands of the Army of the Potomac—which existed during Civil War days. In fact, in response to defending himself against having been chiefly responsible for Custer's defeat and death by failing to come to his assistance in his greatest hour of need, Benteen was only pointing out the Custer-Eliza relationship, which he had kept secret by him for nearly twenty years, to challenge the stainless Custer image and his canonization by the media and public.

After all, this excessive glorification of Custer had strayed far from the more mundane realities and facts that have so sharply diverged from the much-touted "saintliness" of Custer, while coming at the proud Virginian's expense as an officer, including as a Civil War hero, and a gentleman.

Like all men with strengths and weaknesses, Custer was certainly no perfect man and soldier as portrayed by Elizabeth in her three books and as emphasized by writers and the American press for generations. Benteen merely pointed out the sharp contradictions to the idealized Custer myth, which came at his expense because he had become a scapegoat, like Marcus Albert Reno who also was a Civil War veteran, for the disaster at the Little Bighorn.[120]

Indeed, Benteen had only pointed basic truths about Custer and his life by emphasizing the most obvious blemishes that contradicted the romantic myth of Custer, and Eliza was just the most prominent blemish in his Southern mind. The captain certainly had an axe to grind.

Indeed, while Custer was endlessly glorified to no end by an adorning American public for an extended period, Benteen gained the lion's share of blame for Custer's demise at the Little Bighorn, because of his tardy arrival of his three companies in rejoining Reno's contingent of three companies, which had been defeated before Custer and his men of five companies had gone down fighting on the high ground that overlooked the Little Bighorn River in one of the most remote sections of the sprawling Montana Territory.

In truth and as noted, Benteen was a hero of the Civil War because of his bravery and his popularity with the rank and file was extremely high, which continued unabated when serving in the 7th Cavalry. However, Captain Benteen's reputation was forever stained, thanks partly to Elizabeth's popular books, and creation of an enduring American myth in the Custer mystique, which meant that the fundamental truths about Benteen and his words, especially about Eliza, had to be systematically and casually discarded.

Indeed, generations of pro-Custer historians, writers, and journalists have simply never looked closely into Benteen's charges when it came to the privileged "Queen of Sheba," dismissing them out-of-hand–not unlike the original rumors of Jefferson's relationship with Sally Hemings which were long dismissed by so many leading Americans of the historical community--, because they failed to fit the highly-sanitized and romanticized image of Custer.

Of course, any mention of a possible Custer-Eliza relationship by writers or historians would have disgraced Elizabeth and badly-tarnished the highly-romanticized Custer-Libbie relationship and marriage that had been elevated to a Victorian Era model of perfection in every way to the disgust of Benteen and others, who had intimately known Custer's other side.[121]

As mentioned, after Custer's death in late June 1876, Libbie was largely responsible for protecting her husband's memory against his critics, and fueling the romantic idealization that bolstered the Custer myth, which had no room for a black woman and former slave named Eliza Denison Brown. As mentioned, among the chief critics of Custer was Benteen, who desired to clear his name for the Little Bighorn disaster by revealing what he knew to have been true.

The captain and native Southerner was immensely popular with his men because of his leadership skills and gallantry long demonstrated by him in battle, and in the eyes of a good many of 7th Cavalry survivors, who blamed Custer for the Little Bighorn defeat. As a Southerner, Benteen was far less likely to have worshipped at the alter of his old 7th Cavalry commander

However, Benteen's emphasis on a Custer-Eliza sexual relationship that spanned the course of two wars in regions separated by more than 1,500 miles has been long dismissed by historians primarily because the proud captain has been generally blamed for failing to rush to Custer's aid at the Battle of the Little Big Horn and then fought back with words against the all-powerful Custer myth and Elizabeth's endless idealization of her husband.

As mentioned, the mysteries about what had exactly happened at the Little Bighorn and why have played a large part in allowing for Custer's greatest secret to have been forgotten and having only emerged at this late date. According to the accepted version of events, Benteen allegedly allowed his commander and his men to die out of spite and jealousy, and his post-Little Bighorn words, especially about Eliza, were seen in the same light. As mentioned, Benteen and Reno, who had been defeated and unnerved in the battle by the time of Benteen's arrival, emerged as the primary villains of the Little Bighorn fiasco in the American press and in the public mind.

Custerphiles have long embraced this traditional scenario of the Battle of Little Bighorn to preserve the glorified memory of Custer, who should have lived to fight another day in their minds, if only Benteen, along with Reno, had reinforced their commander and his five companies in a timely manner during the "Last Stand."

Therefore, if generations of historians and scholars found truth in Benteen's charges of a Custer-Eliza relationship that mocked the saintly imaged of Custer which had been created by Elizabeth in her books and society's much touted perfection of a Victorian Age romance, then perhaps he was telling the truth in explaining his inability to aid Custer in time, when his own and Reno's troopers (both commanded three 7th Cavalry companies while Custer commanded five companies) were under severe attack by a large number of Sioux and Cheyenne warriors during the defense of Reno Hill, which was located on the Little Bighorn far south of Custer's position on the high ground farther downriver.

Ideal Relationship

However, some of the best evidence of the secret existence of the Custer-Eliza relationship was that it was an ideal overall situation for Custer, especially after the dangerous Anna E. Jones liaison, which had almost proved a complete disaster that might well have ended his promising career and perhaps even his relationship with Libbie had she learned of the ugly details about Custer's lust for a sexy teenager.[122]

Therefore, for sexual fulfillment, Custer needed an attractive woman in his midst at headquarters and one who posed no threat by telling no tales like the trouble-making Anna, and Eliza was a certain guarantee that whatever went on between them would remain a secret. Since Eliza depended on Custer from the beginning and felt affection and respect for him, then these were two fundamental reasons why she would not tell anyone about their secret sexual relationship.

Even more, Eliza was illiterate like most slaves, which also guaranteed a hushed silence. Custer, consequently, had no need to fear anything from the written word by way of the hand of Eliza, unlike Anna, that might have resulted in an investigation like in Anna's case, which had caused supreme embarrassment to the young man of such outstanding promise.

Just as Thomas Jefferson found "in one sense the perfect mate" in young, beautiful Sally Hemings, so Custer found much the same in an attractive, good-natured, and humorous Eliza Brown. Like on the isolated hilltop of Monticello and in regard to Custer's headquarters during the Civil War years, a former slave mistress remained in the hazy background far from any kind of serious scrutiny to ensure no scandal in the white army establishment would erupt to reach high levels, especially in a chaotic wartime environment of the Cavalry Corps of the Army of the Potomac.

With a war to fight, the fact that Eliza served at headquarters at a time when large numbers of blacks filled domestic roles for Union officers throughout the war was only part of the norm in a wartime environment, providing an effective smokescreen.

Even more, the question of marriage would never be an issue, requirement, or concern for either Jefferson or Custer, even if they fell in love because the woman of their choice was a slave or an ex-slave, respectively. Quite simply, a slave or former slave woman offered the possibility of a relatively easy and stressless intimate relationship, purely sexual or loving, or both, without any strings attached, and, most important, without risking one's reputation, career, or status, because these women of the lowest class in America were all but guaranteed to be discreet and could be trusted with keeping a secret.[123]

Consequently, in the end, the worst repercussions suffered by Custer because of his close relationship with Eliza were the flow of camp gossip and rumors that flew along the soldier's grapevine about "the Queen of Sheba," which was a relatively small price to pay. Most important as far as Custer was concerned, an intimate relationship with Eliza would never become official army scandal with a possible investigation and Custer having to answer sensitive questions asked by prudish and self-righteous superiors like in the recent case with sex-pot Anna E. Jones. Clearly, Custer had learned his lesson the hard way, and he would not make the same mistake twice now that he had been a newly-appointed brigadier general and had become a hero of Gettysburg, where the tide of the war had turned in a decisive way.

In fact and as noted, Custer's relationship with a young, attractive black woman might even have been even enhanced his popularity to some degree among his jaunty young cavalrymen, who took sex where he found it, black or white, when campaigning or in camp in the Napoleonic Era tradition. In the end, the reputation for male virility and stamina only enhanced Custer's dynamic image as a powerful warrior, an aggressive cavalry commander, and a bold young man of conquest, both and off the battlefield.[124]

Custer's Own Words

The depth of affection and the visible close relationship between Custer and Eliza was also partly revealed by the fact that she was able to openly tease Custer, who was noted for his large ego and thin skin, like few others, such as family members. In 1864 because she knew him so well, possessed a cutting sense of humor, and thought quite differently from most others less grounded in common sense born of the slave experience, Eliza even taunted Custer in mocking fashion about his lofty image among his troopers: "Why, Gin'ral, the men think you can do as much as the Almighty!"[125]

Likewise, Custer greatly admired Eliza for her many redeeming personal qualities, including her slave-based humor and witticisms that were prominent features of African-American culture and the slave community. However, Custer most of all admired Eliza's deep devotion to him. In a June 21, 1864 letter to his wife and as mentioned, Custer described "Eliza [as] faithful to the last!"[126]

Even more revealing, Eliza openly teased Custer about his relationship with his wife and quite unlike anyone else was able to do. As Custer wrote in a March 30, 1865 letter to Libbie, he described how during the advance on Dinwiddie Court House, located just southwest of Petersburg, Virginia, in pursuit of Lee's reeling Army of Northern Virginia, which was on the dismal road to its final surrender at Appomattox Court House only a week and a half, how, "Last night I slept on the ground by the roadside, the rain coming down in torrents, our wagons several miles in the rear [and] My only protection was the fine rubber poncho [and] For a pillow I had a stick laid across two parallel rails. Before I got the rails I slept a little, then woke to find myself in a puddle about two inches deep . . . When the wagons came and I told Eliza about it she said, 'Oh, I 'spect you wanted Miss Libbie with you . . . . and she just as willing, and she'd have said, 'Oh, isn't this nice!'"[127]

With a sharp sense of humor that had been well-honed in the overall experience of coping with the living nightmare of slavery to deal with adversity in the face of an oppressive system and which was a longtime product of the slave community and the black experience in general, Eliza was in part hinting of Custer and his wife sleeping together and making love, which would have been "nice."[128]

Indeed, Eliza was alluding to the act of love, joking how the ardent Custer would have eagerly made love to Elizabeth even in the pouring rain, almost as if she personally knew some of the exact details about the energetic, youthful general's sexual libido and appetite, which was quite high, from personal experience.

This situation was no exaggeration because Custer's hyperactive sexual appetite and libido was partly revealed in a March 1865 letter to Libbie from White House, Virginia, when he emphasized his "sexual yearning" for Elizabeth, and even prominently mentioned his male organ and his desire to perform oral sex upon her, which she obviously relished in the bedroom.

As Custer penned with surprising openness for a Civil War general to have written to his wife in a letter, which could always be captured and exploited by the Confederates to his supreme embarrassment: "I am longing and anxiously hoping for the time to come when I can be with my darling little one again [as] It seems so long since I saw her and had 'Just one.' I do not think the squirrel you sent me can satisfy the want and cravings of 'our mutual friend.' What would I not give Just for one kiss from those dear lips." Of course, "our mutual friend" was an obvious reference to Custer's penis that Elizabeth had evidently grown to love during the couple's most intimate moments.[129]

During this same period, Custer penned another letter to Libbie that was even more graphic in terms of sexual content. On a Sunday and instead of listing to the self-righteous words of a boring camp sermon from an army chaplain, Custer was thinking about sex, including the oral sex that he desired to bestow upon Libbie for her pleasure. He wrote in no uncertain and most revealing terms how, "Oh I do want so badly. I know *where* I would kiss somebody if I was with her tonight."[130]

In much the same way as Eliza had joked with her beloved "Ginnil," Custer returned the jests with sexually-laden references and humor, joking with Eliza in much the same way that he was also open about the subject of sex with his wife in his letters. Custer was no prude, sexual or otherwise, despite his high rank, West Point education, and winning ways on the battlefield.

Custer's fun-loving nature and often almost boyish personality were unconventional and contrarian, and he was very much of an unorthodox individual—a true maverick-- both on and off the battlefield. Most of all, Custer's personality was distinguished by an open, free-spiritedness, and humorous nature–which reflected his family's love of horseplay and upbringing in which practical jokes between his Ohio father, Emanuel Henry Custer who had been born in 1806, and his fun-loving sons continued unabated well into adulthood, and even while Custer led the 7th Cavalry on the Great Plains--, when he was not in the dignified pose of a highly-respected general officer and in his private moments.

Because it was part of his fun-loving nature, Custer was surprisingly open about the subject of sex that was relatively rare among the usual writings left behind by Civil War soldiers, especially generals, in their letters. As revealed in a February 9, 1869 letter to his wife and again revealing that Eliza was often on his mind and displaying affection for her almost like a father, Custer wrote: "Tell Eliza I have a [buffalo] robe for her, one of those presented [by the Indians] to me . . . ."[131]

But perhaps what was more significant about this passage was that in the previous sentence, Custer had reminded Elizabeth that, "To-day is our wedding anniversary [and] I am sorry we cannot spend it together, but I shall celebrate it in my heart."[132]

While Custer planned to celebrate his wedding anniversary in his heart, he was also thinking about Eliza and a nice gift for her to reveal the extent of his affection for her. Ironically, he mentioned no effort to obtain an anniversary gift for Libbie in this February 9, 1869 letter in which he emphasized that Eliza was going to receive a special gift from him, because he knew that she would treasure such a personal item.[133]

Perhaps most of all and revealed in previous examples of the Custer's thoughtful nature when it came to the former slave, Eliza never seemed to have been far from Custer's thoughts, even in letters to his wife as noted. On June 28, 1864 from an encampment on the "south side of the James River, ten miles below City Point, Virginia," Custer penned to Elizabeth in the opening sentences of his short letter: "I am seated on the river bank [and] Eliza is near her tent, giving utterance to her peculiar and sage remarks. My tent is [near Eliza's tent and] under a beautiful, widespreading tree on a bluff [while] The men are camped beneath." Clearly, Custer and Eliza possessed a degree of personal privacy in this special place amid a wooded bivouac area, while encamped on the river bluff and away from the main army encampment that was noisy and busy.[134]

Then, by November 1864, Eliza's quarters had been expanded in size to a private tent, which was so large that it served "for dining-room" for Custer and his closest associates, or staff members, and, of course, including Libbie when he visited the encampment and her husband.[135]

Custer gained so much confidence in Eliza that when he wrote to Libbie's father, Judge Daniel S. Bacon of Monroe, Michigan, in November 1864 from his headquarters in the Shenandoah Valley at Winchester, Virginia, while serving under the command of General "Little Phil" Sheridan, he comforted the judge about his daughter's welfare when his command moved out to face the enemy by writing: "Libbie will be left in a safe a comfortable place near the main body of the army [and with] Eliza with her" for protection.[136]

As repeatedly demonstrated, Custer's supreme trust in Eliza's role in protecting and safeguarding his beloved wife, which existed for years during the Civil War, was faithfully continued in the Indian Wars. Just before riding off to engage in duty against Native Americans on the Great Plains, Custer yelled to Eliza, "Take care of Libbie, Eliza."[137]

As mentioned, the notable fact that Eliza was never far from Custer's thoughts and feelings can be seen when he often mentioned her in letters to his wife, and his words betrayed a great deal about the closeness of the two. This deep affection can been seen when Custer wrote from Fort Hays, Kansas, which was located about halfway between Kansas City and the Rocky Mountains, on May 1, 1867: "Tell Eliza I am in search of an Indian husband for her–one who won't bother her to sew buttons on his shirts and pants, nor would his washing be heavy. And one dish at a meal would satisfy him."[138]

Of course, Custer was referring to himself, and his relationship with Eliza and the demands that he put on her, like sewing on buttons, cooking, washing, etc. Custer's words also revealed a hint of subliminal flirtation about husband status, male superiority, and the act of sex like Eliza's own flirtatious words to him about Libbie and sex.[139]

When Eliza later said that she "jined up with the Ginnil" on that hot late July 1863 day in Rappahannock County, Virginia, these words very likely possessed more than one meaning, considering the subsequent course of events in regard to a close relationship that had been forged and then blossomed between the two.[140]

In psychological terms and in truth, Custer possessed a host of long-overlooked personal qualities that had made an extremely close and intimate relationship with Eliza all but inevitable for a variety of reasons. Most of all and as noted, Custer was relatively enlightened in matters of race, especially when it came to attractive women who he found appealing, and he displayed no prejudice at all in this regard. As Custer wrote in a July 1865 letter from Alexandria, Louisiana, to his father-in-law Judge Bacon who had once been a respected member of the state legislature of Michigan, when the 7th Cavalry was serving as part of the occupying force during Reconstruction: "This country is wholly unlike Virginia. It is more like notions formed from [Harriet Beecher Stowe's famous anti-slavery novel] 'Uncle Tom's Cabin.' Slavery was not as mild as" in the border states, like Maryland and Kentucky, and even in Virginia that Custer had learned about during the Civil War years.

Sickened by what he saw and learned about slavery in this part of Louisiana, Custer described the horror of this plantation world in the Deep South, where "slaves [were] at the mercy of their owners, in the Red River country, and every plantation had its Simon Legree and humble Uncle

Tom. In the mansion where I now write is a young negro woman whose back bears the scars of five hundred lashes give at one time, for going beyond the limits of her master's plantation. If the War has attained nothing else it has placed America under a debt of gratitude for all time, for [the] removal of this evil."[141]

Eliza's End As a "Custer Family" Member

After serving with Custer and Elizabeth on the Great Plains since the formation to the 7th Cavalry and after Custer had taken command of the regiment during the summer of 1866, the year of 1869 was destined to be the last that Eliza was to part of the Custer "family."[142]

Perhaps Libbie's suspicions were almost certainly aroused because she took a keener notice of her husband's attitude and conduct toward Eliza, including perhaps Custer's February 9, 1869 letter to Libbie in which he reminded her of their wedding anniversary and mentioned that he had "a [buffalo] role for her" and nothing for his wife.[143]

At some point in 1869 and as revealed by Captain Benteen, Elizabeth might have discovered that Custer and Eliza either had a relationship in the past or perhaps it had even continued to exist in some form or that it perhaps even had been rekindled in terms of intimacy.[144] Over the years, Elizabeth also certainly had her own mounting suspicions about such "derelictions," in Benteen's words.

After all, Eliza had been the only women around Custer for years, especially when he had campaigned in the field for nearly half of 1863, all of 1864, and the first four months of 1865. And, of course, Custer and Eliza had grown together as persons and ever-closer in terms of their relationship from their wartime experiences year after year.

And Libbie, when visiting the Union encampment to see her husband, had seen the close interaction between the general and former slave, and the fact that their tents were often located close together in the encampment at night: a situation that was much like Jefferson's bedroom having been located not far from Sally Heming's quarters at Monticello for easy access and secret activities of a sexual nature.

As noted, Custer had written at least one letter that revealed the close proximity of Eliza's tent to his own tent that might have caused some suspicions in Elizabeth's mind, but probably not. What could not be denied was the fact that Eliza was no old, unsightly hag, but a young, vibrant, healthy, and athletic black women, who was "comely" in the description of one white historian, who was guilty of understating the case.[145]

For a trusting and naive Elizabeth, who was a small town product and had been isolated in an upper-class cocoon while growing-up in Monroe, all of these past memories, references, hints, and subtle indications of an intimate relationship between Custer and Eliza might have now come back to her haunt in the end.

If so, then these certainly once-ignored clues and hints would have hit her like a body-blow, leaving Elizabeth in some shock. After all when younger and thinner in her younger days, Elizabeth had been the belle of Monroe and possessed no rivals in your youthful glory and glowing radiance, when she had been in her prime years ago.

In consequence, any indications of impropriety between her husband and a former slave would have been especially jolting to Elizabeth in purely psychological terms, because they thoroughly mocked the values of her upper-class world in which she had long existed on a pedestal. After all, Eliza had been a close friend and a faithful member of the Custer "family" year after year, while holding the complete trust of Custer and Elizabeth.

Over the years, a wide variety of excuses have been offered by historians for Eliza's abrupt departure that was unceremonious and hasty. And only one person of the family possessed the will and power of dismissal to seal Eliza's fate, which caused a hasty exit from "the family."

Eliza was dismissed by Elizabeth, evidently in an angry, jealous rage that was certainly understandable under the circumstances, if indications of some kind of intimacy between her and her husband had been ascertained by the good wife.

After all, Eliza had betrayed Elizabeth's trust in the end, but never Custer's esteem and affection, because he remained her greatest supporter. However, Custer had no choice but to bow to Elizabeth's unliteral decision to remove Eliza and banish her from the little "family."

Nevertheless, this sudden separation was a painful one for all concerned. It is not known and as mentioned but the very real possibility existed that Elizabeth had looked back in the past and remembered old signs and obvious hints that she had ignored, because the mere thought of a possible intimate relationship between Custer and Eliza had seemed so utterly impossible, since they were more like friends and even brother and sister in some basic ways.

What cannot be denied was the fact that Eliza and Elizabeth had been extremely close, sharing a good deal together over a period of more than half a decade. Libbie had written to her father on May 1, 1864 from the nation's capital, while Custer and Eliza had remained in the Army of the Potomac's cavalry encampment in Virginia, because of the new spring campaign had been underway: "I did not write you half enough about Eliza when I was in camp. She is a jewel of a servant."[146]

Then, in another letter, written from Winchester, Virginia, on November 13, 1864 when Custer was serving under General Sheridan, Libbie loved to be served by hyper-attentive blacks, including Eliza, who she realized were vastly superior to white servants in their overall attentiveness and duties. Sounding almost like a proper Southern Belle of the aristocracy and from the plantation world of the Deep South because she was a northern upper-class product like the slave-owning ladies of the South, Libbie had been convinced that black men and women made the best servants to cater to her whims. Consequently, she wrote about her revelation with some excitement: "Mother, if once you had colored servants you would never want any other."[147]

Unlike her husband's accepting, open, and playful boyish ways, and affectionate interaction with Eliza, this typical upper-class and condescending attitude of Elizabeth, the pampered and spoiled daughter of a respected judge and who referred to blacks in her diary as darkies, might also have also played a part in having motivate Eliza in her desire to have embarked upon a relationship with Libbie's husband at some point: of course, the best revenge for demeaning treatment based upon a sense of white superiority and entitlement, if that was the case.

Of course, this kind of possible motivation for Eliza's actions is not known because of the lack of historical documentation and is nothing more than speculation given the circumstances. However, this distinct possibly certainly does exist because Elizabeth was a true aristocrat with blueblood ways from her upbringing in a wealthy family and as the judge's only daughter and Eliza was on the receiving end of an air of superiority for year after year.

Revealing a degree of defiance, Eliza sometimes openly mocked Elizabeth and her elitist white attitudes of the upper-class when she was not around as in the case of so many slaves in their master's absence that became a permanent part of black culture, mimicking her voice, talk, and sentiment as silly, including when with her beloved Custer in regard to romance and his sexual ways.[148]

At the war's end and noted, it was also revealing that when Custer left the Army of the Potomac and journeyed to Washington, D.C., to muster out of service in early March

1866, he had taken Eliza with him. Elizabeth, meanwhile, had been sent back to her family in far-away Monroe.

In time, Custer belatedly dispatched Eliza west but only after Elizabeth specifically requested for Eliza to be sent by her husband to join her in Monroe just so that she could be catered to and served like a queen. However, was Elizabeth suspicious about the true nature of the Custer-Eliza relationship at this time, explaining why she had decided to have recalled Eliza, since Judge Bacon already had his own servants in the house where his daughter stayed?

What was significant was the fact that Eliza had not accompanied Libbie back to Monroe, and instead had gone east to Washington, D.C., to be by the side of Custer, who still needed the "Queen of Sheba," instead of having been sent west with his wife.[149]

But perhaps most revealing of all was Eliza's emotional reaction to Custer's return from dangerous duty on the Great Plains. When Custer had unexpectedly appeared at Fort Riley and surprised Libbie by his sudden presence from ever-risky of service against Native Americans, "Eliza, half crying, scolding as she did when overjoyed, vibrated between kitchen and parlor, and finally fell to cooking, as a safety-value for her overcharged spirits."[150]

And significantly, Libbie wrote about this revealing episode with much understatement, without suspecting the true depth of the feeling and strong emotions that Eliza held deep inside for her husband, although they were openly displayed by the former slave on this occasion. Clearly, in many ways, Eliza's uncontrollable emotional reaction was much like that of a wife or lover, because of the open exhibition of the true depth of her emotional response to Custer's sudden appearance.

After she had been dismissed from the family by Elizabeth, the fate of Eliza has been a mysterious one for an extended period, before she married a southern Ohio lawyer named Brown and lived a long life. Most likely after her sudden dismissal by Elizabeth, she initially remained in the West that this former slave woman had grown to love over the years.

If so, then she would have followed in the footsteps of Cathy Williams, a former Missouri slave who had disguised herself as a male to serve for nearly two years in a Buffalo Soldier regiment in the West. Cathy had then settled down in the small community of Trinidad, Colorado, where she finally found her piece of paradise on the western frontier and far from the former land of slavery.

For the record, this current author was the first one who told the remarkable story of the life of his former slave in his 2002 book *Cathy Williams, From Slave to Female Buffalo Soldier*, which was published by Stackpole Publishing. This groundbreaking book shed a good deal of new light on the experience of a young woman in slavery, the Civil War years when connected with Union Armies like Eliza, and her service in 38th United States Infantry as a Buffalo Soldier, after having enlisted on November 15, 1866 at Jefferson Barracks, Missouri.[151]

But what cannot be in doubt or linger as a mystery was the certain reality that Eliza Denison Brown broke down and cried her eyes out when she learned about the death of George Armstrong Custer at the Little Bighorn on June 25, 1876. She had lost someone who she dearly loved to the very end.

Epilogue

For the record and as previously noted, this current book was not written in any attempt to defame or stain the image of a genuine American hero, but to give Custer new life as a person and to reveal a forgotten, but important, aspect of his life not previously the subject of a book. This current author's past works, including *Custer at Gettysburg, A New Look at George Armstrong Custer versus Jeb Stuart in the Battle's Climactic Cavalry Charges* (Stackpole Books, 2019) and other books, have praised Custer for his battlefield feats, skills, and accomplishments at considerable length.

Most of all, therefore, this current book was created in the hope of telling a forgotten story that needed to be revealed at long last, while presenting a fresh perspective and adding a new understanding about one of the most famous military figures in American history and one of the most obscure figures in history, Eliza Denison Brown.

For the first time, consequently, the Custer-Eliza relationship has not only revealed the more human and intimate side of one of America's most famous Civil War heroes, but also his better, or more affectionate, side as well: the forgotten Custer who had been long lost to the historical record and long thought to have been virtually nonexistent.

After all and to his great credit during an age when anti-black sentiment was exceptionally high, Custer treated a former slave from Virginia and young black woman with a sense of admiration, respect, and equality that was rare for the day from a white man of high status and privilege.

Therefore, all existing evidence has indicated that there was absolutely nothing either exploitative or abusive in the Custer-Eliza relationship, which was one of mutual consent that existed between two individuals, who felt admiration and considerable affection toward each other, as revealed by their words and actions for years.

In fact, this close wartime relationship, which existed in two wars, was the very antithesis of an abusive or exploitative relationship with Eliza. After all, Custer had been born in the North within the warm cocoon of an egalitarian-minded and humor-focused family, which ensured that he was open-minded in matters of race.[152]

Most important as seen by the severe late twentieth-century white backlash, especially from older and conservative Virginia historians, against the mere thought of a possible intimate Thomas Jefferson–Sally Hemings relationship, despite the existence of primary evidence and secondary documentation that had clearly indicated otherwise, a relationship with a black women–be it Custer or a sensitive founding father on a remote Virginia mountaintop–does absolutely nothing to bring disgrace or damage the overall image of Custer or anyone else for that matter simply because of the sole factor of race.

In truth, a mutual intimate relationship with a former slave does not blacken Custer's reputation any more than that of America's third president who had loved Sally Hemings on his revered hilltop at Monticello located just outside Charlottesville, Virginia, because all existing evidence has indicated that these two relationships (Custer-Eliza Denison Brown and Jefferson—Sally Hemings) in the same state, Virginia, were based on mutual consent and respect.

My overall purpose in the writing of this current book has been only to pierce the heavy fog of seemingly endless glorification and mythology about America's most famous cavalier to see though the layers of the romantic image and facade to catch a rare glimpse of Custer as a real being and human being.

And, most of all, this ambitious goal of this current author has been to tell for the first time the long-forgotten story about how and why two remarkable individuals–one black, one white–had suddenly and accidently come together as one in wartime and related to each other very much as equals in the rarest of developments at this time, despite their vast differences in class, background, culture, and, of course, race, while under the stress and dangers of America's bloodiest war.

During America's greatest national trial and modern Iliad that had lasted from 1861 to 1865, a white Civil War hero of the American nation and people, George Armstrong Custer, a real man of passion and not the stereotypical pure and ultra-romantic knight of a bygone age, and Eliza Brown, a former Virginia slave who was in search of a new life, unexpectedly came together because they had viewed each other as fellow human beings with mutual admiration and respect at a time, when the overall process of dehumanization of America's bloodiest conflict reached new heights.

Because of this heightened degree of mutual admiration and respect that never ended between the two, Custer and

Eliza were able to come together as one in wartime to share a life together in a headquarters environment for an extended period under the most difficult and challenging circumstances, when the America nation was struggling for its existence.

In the beginning, a strange fate, twisting destiny, and the fortunes of war had united an escaped female slave from the Virginia Piedmont and a white Union general from Ohio to forge a wartime a team at a time, when American was searching for its own meaning and self-identity during the turbulent 1860s in the most brutal war in the annals of American history.

In much the same way and about the same time, so young Custer and Eliza were also looking for their respective places in the world that had seemingly gone crazy with Americans killing fellow Americans as rapidly as possible for what they believed was right. This searing wartime experience profoundly shaped the lives of Custer and Eliza Brown in ways that neither could have imagined or believed possible only shortly before their respective destinies were changed forever by the war and a chance meeting amid the picturesque Virginia Piedmont.

During some of the most arduous and bloodiest campaigns of the Civil War and both on and off the battlefield in two wars across a wide front on both sides of the Mississippi River, Custer and Eliza shared a special bond, affection, and mutual respect that was fully displayed and recognized by many others, especially the boys in blue, for years and one that was seldom seen between one of the most popular military men in America and an obscure female slave from the Old Dominion. In many ways, Custer and Eliza were truly soul mates on a special level to forge an unique bond not enjoyed by Elizabeth.

In the end and as a strange fate would have it for comparable reasons, Elizabeth Clift Bacon-Custer, an upper-class blueblood from Monroe, Michigan, and Eliza, a lowly house slave from a lonely plantation in Rappahannock County, Virginia, were forever traumatized by the awful name of Little Bighorn and its tragic implications for the dynamic man, who they both loved. Given all the available historical evidence, Eliza Denison Brown was indeed Custer's forgotten soulmate in not one but two wars during one of the most turbulent periods in the annals of American history.

About the Author

PHILLIP THOMAS TUCKER, Ph.D., has won international acclaim on both sides of the Atlantic as today's leading "New Look" historian, who has authored a large number of "New Look" books of unique distinction. Throughout his career as a professional historian, he has focused on a wide variety of unique aspects of the African American experience to reveal its full richness and complexities, while bestowing long-overdue recognition to forgotten men and women. The *Haitian Revolutionary Women Series* (3 volumes), the *New Look Glory 54th Massachusetts Series* (4 volumes), *Harriet Tubman Series* (5 volumes), and *Cathy Williams Series* (3 volumes) have continued the author's long-existing tradition of bestowing well-deserved recognition and praising the impressive achievements of remarkable African Americans, men and women, throughout the annals of American history. One of America's most prolific and groundbreaking historians, Tucker has authored nearly 70 highly-original books to reveal long-ignored and silenced chapters of history, while correcting the historical record for the twenty-first century.

Notes

[1]"Twilight of Slavery, 'Enlightened' Accommodations No Match for Freedom," Rappahannock County, Virginia, Historic Marker; Margerite Merington, editor, *The Custer Story, The Life and Intimate Letters of General Custer and His Wife Elizabeth*, (New York: The Devin-Adair Company, n.d. 1950), pp. 61, 178; Kenneth M. Stampp, *The Peculiar Institution, Slavery in the Ante-Bellum South*, (New York: Vintage Books, 1956), p. 18

[2]Edmund S. Morgan, *American Slavery, American Freedom, The Ordeal of Colonial Virginia*, (New York: W. W. Norton and Company, Inc., 1975), pp. 105-387; Robert William Fogel and Stanley L. Engerman, *Time On the Cross, The Economics of American Negro Slavery*, (New York: Little, Brown and Company, 1974), p. 44; Stampp, *The Peculiar Institution*, pp. 18, 48-49, 51; Annette Gordon-Reed, *The Hemingses of Monticello, An American Family*, (New York: W. W. Norton and Company, 2008), pp. 23-32.

[3]Morgan, *American Slavery, American Freedom*, p. 387; Fogel and Engerman, *Time On the Cross*, p. 3; Eric Foner, *Forever Free, The Story of Emancipation and Reconstruction*, (New York: Alfred A. Knopf, 2005), pp. 7-9, 11-13; Jeffry D. Wert, *Custer, The Controversial Life of George Armstrong Custer*, (New York: Simon and Schuster, 1997), p. 106; Wendy Warren, *New England Bound, Slavery and Colonization in Early America*, (New York: Liveright Publishing Corporation, 2016), pp. 1-185.

[4]"Twilight of Slavery 'Enlightened' Accommodations No Match for Freedom," *RCHM*; Merlington, ed., *The Custer Story*, pp. 61, 178; Wert, *Custer*, p. 106; Ohio Academy Medical History Presentation, "Dr. Noah Elliott, African American Pioneer, by Carl J. Denbow, PhD; Deborah Fitts, "Rappahannock County to Get Markers, Join State Civil War Trials," *Civil War News*,

(November 2007); Ben Venue, African American Historic Site Databases, Virginia Foundation for the Humanities, website, internet; Phillip Thomas Tucker, *Custer at Gettysburg, A New Look at George Armstrong Custer versus Jeb Stuart in the Battle's Climactic Cavalry Charges*, (Guilford: Stackpole Books, 2019), pp. 159-235.

[5]Wert, *Custer*, p. 106; Merington, ed., *The Custer Story*, p. 178; "Twilight of Slavery 'Enlightened' Accommodations No Match for Freedom," *RCHM.*

[6]Elizabeth B. Custer, *Tenting on the Plains, General Custer in Kansas and Texas*, (New York: Barnes and Noble, 2006), p. 283.

[7]Wert, *Custer*, pp. 106-107; Merington, ed., *The Custer Story*, p. 178.

[8]John W. Blassingame, *The Slave Community, Plantation Life in the Antebellum South*, (New York: Oxford University Press, 1972), p. 77.

[9]Blassingame, *The Slave Community*, pp. 27-103; Wert, *Custer*, pp. 106-107; Merington, ed., *The Custer Story*, p. 108.

[10]Blassingame, *The Slave Community*, pp. 27-103; Wert, *Custer*, p. 106; "Twilight of Slavery 'Enlightened' Accommodations No Match for Freedom," *RCHM*; Merington, ed., *The Custer Story*, 178; Phillip Thomas Tucker, *From Auction Block to Glory, The African American Experience*, (New York: Metro Books, 1998), pp. 1-71, 88-122 ; Ron Field, *Avenging Angel, John Brown's Raid on Harpers Ferry 1859*, (Oxford: Osprey Publishing Ltd., 2012), p. 30.

[11]Wert, *Custer*, p. 106; Merington, ed., *The Custer Story*, p. 178; Custer, *Tenting on the Plains*, pp. 10, 283; Ed Longacre, Custer and His Wolverines, (Conshohocken: Combined Publishing, 1997), pp. 178-179; Tucker, *Custer at Gettysburg*, pp. 159-385.

[12]Wert, *Custer*, p. 106; Longacre, *Custer and His Wolverines*, pp. 178-179.

[13]Foner, *Forever Free*, p. 14.

14Nell Irvin Painter, *Creating Black Americans, African-American History and Its Meanings, 1619 to Present*, (New York: Oxford University Press, 2006), p. 92.

15"Twilight of Slavery 'Enlightened' Accomodations No Match for Freedom," *RCHM*; George Armstrong Custer July 23 and July 24, 1863 reports to Major General Alfred Pleasonton, "Draw the Sword," Gettysburg Monument Project, website, internet; Merington, ed., *The Custer Story*, p. 61; Wert, *Custer*, p. 106; Ben Venue, African American Heritage Sites Databases, Virginia, FH; Mary Elizabeth Hite, My Rappahannock (Va.) Storybook, (Richmond: Dietz Press, 1950), pp. 206-209; Longacre, *Custer and his Wolverines*, pp. 178-179.

16Wert, *Custer*, p. 106; Custer July 24, 1863 report to Major General Pleasanton, "Draw the Sword," GMP; Longacre, *Custer and his Wolverines*, pp. 178-179.

17Custer July 23, 24, and 25 reports to Major General Pleasanton, "Draw the Sword," GMP; Wert, Custer, p. 106; Deborah Fitts, "Rappahannock County to Get Markers, Join State Civil War Trails," (Nov. 2007), internet; Spindle House for sale, Zillow, internet; Longacre, *Custer and his Wolverines*, pp. 178-181; Custer, *Tenting on the Plains*, p. 10.

18Custer, *Tenting on the Plains*, p. 10.

19Ibid.

20Ibid.

21Hite, *My Rappahannock (Va.) Storybook*, pp. 206-209; Wert, *Custer*, p. 206; Custer July 23, 24, and 25 report to Major General Pleasanton, "Draw the Sword," GMP; Fitts, "Rappahannock County to Get Markers, Join State Civil War Trails," internet; Longacre, *Custer and his Wolverines*, pp. 130-131; Tucker, *Custer at Gettysburg*, pp. 159-385.

22Custer, *Tenting on the Plains*, p. 10.

23Wert, *Custer*, p. 106; Custer, *Tenting on the Plains*, pp. 10, 194.

24Custer, *Tenting on the Plains*, p. 10.

[25]Ibid; Tucker, *Custer at Gettysburg*, pp. 159-385.

[26] Wayne C. Temple, editor, *Campaigning With Grant by General Horace Porter*, (New York: Bonanza Books, 1961), pp. 126-127.

[27]Wert, *Custer*, p. 106; Fitts, "Rappahannock to Get Markers, Join State Civil War Trails," CWN, internet.

[28]Painter, *Creating Black Americans*, p. 109; Custer July 23, 1863 report to Major General Pleasanton, "Draw the Sword," GMP; Fitts,"Rappahannock County to Get Markers, Join State Civil War Trails," CWN.

[29]Wert, *Custer*, p. 106; Painter, *Creating Black Americans*, p. 109; Custer July 23, 24, and 25, 1863, reports to Major General Pleasanton, "Draw the Sword," GMP.

[30]Custer July 23, 1863 report to Major General Pleasanton, "Draw the Sword," GMP.

[31]Custer July 25, 1863 report to Major General Pleasanton, "Draw the Sword," GMP.

[32]Wert, *Custer*, p. 106.

[33]Temple, ed., *Campaigning With Grant*, pp. 505-506; William H. Leckie, *The Buffalo Soldiers, A Narrative of the Negro Cavalry in the West*, (Norman: University of Oklahoma Press, 1967), p. 6; Ulysses S. Grant, *Personal Memoirs of U. S. Grant*, volume 2, (2 vols., New York: Charles L. Webster and Company, 1885), pp. 114-495.

[34]Temple, ed., *Campaigning With Grant*, p. 507.

[35]Merington, ed., *The Custer Story*, p. 146.

[36]Temple, ed., *Campaigning With Grant*, p. 505.

[37]Merlington, ed., *The Custer Story*, pp. 177-178.

[38]Ibid., p. 178.

[39]Merlington, ed., *The Custer Story*, pp. 108, 178; Custer, *Tenting on the Plains*, pp. 10, 283.

[40]Ibid., p. 179.

[41]Ibid., pp. 61, 178; Custer, *Tenting on the Plains*, pp. 10, 283.

[42]Merington, ed., *The Custer Story*, pp. 61, 178.

[43]Ibid., p. 104.

[44]Leckie, *The Buffalo Soldiers*, p. 16.

[45]Libbie Custer to Rebecca Richmond, December 6, 1866, Kansas Historical Society, Topeka, Kansas.

[46] Ibid; Junction City, Kansas, October 21, 1866.

[47]Libbie Custer to Rebecca Richmond, December 6, 1866, KHS.

[48]Ibid.

[49]Ibid.

[50]Ibid.

[51]Ibid; Wert, *Custer*, pp. 106-107.

[52]Leckie, *The Buffalo Soldiers*, p. 6;

[53]*St. Louis Daily Times*, St. Louis, Missouri; January 2, 1876; Phillip Thomas Tucker, *Cathy Williams, From Slave to Female Buffalo Soldier*, (Mechanicsburg: Stackpole Books, 2002), pp. 1-221.

[54]Leckie, *The Buffalo Soldiers*, pp. 7-8, 14-17; D. Alexander Brown, *Grierson's Raid*, (Urbana: University of Illinois Press, 1962), pp. 5-236; Hutton, ed., *Soldiers West*, pp. 157-159.

[55]Hutton, ed., *Soldiers West*, p. 159.

[56]Tucker, *Cathy Williams*, p. 100; Custer, *My Life on the Plains*, pp. 19-43; Hutton, ed., Soldiers West, pp. 102-103, 158.

[57]Custer, *My Life on the Plains*, p. 44; Hutton, ed., *Soldiers West*, pp. 101-103.

[58]Hutton, ed., *Soldiers West*, pp. 102-103.

[59]Ibid., pp. 100-101, 103-111.

[60]Wert, *Custer*, pp. 106-107, 150, 197-198.

[61]Ibid., pp. 106-107.

[62]Thomas P. Lowry, *The Story of Soldiers Wouldn't Tell*, (Mechanicsburg: Stackpole Books, 1994), p. ix.

[63]Lowry, *The Story the Soldiers Wouldn't Tell*, pp. 1-171; Wert, *Custer*, pp. 211-212.

[64]Connell, *Son of the Morning Star*, p. 125; Wert, *Custer*, p. 107.

[65]Wert, *Custer*, pp. 211-212.

[66]Lowry, *The Story the Soldiers Wouldn't Tell*, pp. 1-171; Tucker, *Custer at Gettysburg*, pp. 299-402.

[67]Lowry, *The Story the Soldiers Wouldn't Tell*, pp. 2-5.

[68]Lowry, *The Story the Soldiers Wouldn't Tell*, pp. 154-155; Holmes, Richard, Redcoat, *The British Soldier in the Age of Horse and Musket*, (New York: W. W. Norton and Company, 2002), p. 155.

[69]Lowry, *The Story the Soldiers Wouldn't Tell*, pp. 154-155; Robert I. Cotton, Jr., and Mary Ellen Hayward, *Maryland in the Civil War*, (Baltimore: John Hopkins University Press, 1994), pp. 35-44.

[70]Lowry, *The Story the Soldiers Wouldn't Tell*, pp. 154-155; Stephen D. Engle, *Yankee Dutchman, The Life of Franz Sigel*, (Fayetteville: The University of Arkansas Press, 1993), pp. 2-4, 32, 37, 43, 50-121, 146-147.

[71]Lowry, *The Story the Soldiers Wouldn't Tell*, p. 154.

[72]Ibid; Engel, *Yankee Dutchman*, p. 147.

[73]Lowry, *The Story the Soldiers Wouldn't Tell*, pp. 154-155.

[74]Lowry, *The Story the Soldiers Wouldn't Tell*, pp. 143-145, 154.

[75]Ibid., pp. 154-155.

[76]Ibid., p. 154.

[77]Ibid.

[78]Ibid., pp. 154-155.

[79]Ibid., p. 155; Garrison, *Amazing Women of the Civil War*, pp. 166-172.

[80]Merington, ed., *The Custer Story*, p. 155.

[81]Ibid., p. 154.

[82]Ibid.

[83]Lowry, *The Story the Soldier Wouldn't Tell*, pp. 1-176.

[84]Ibid., p. 84.

[85]Custer, *Tenting on the Plains*, p. 10.

[86]Ibid., p. 194.

[87]Ibid.

[88]Custer, Tenting on the Plains, p. 298.

[89]Ibid., p. 10

[90]Gordon-Reed, *The Hemingses of Monticello*, pp. 106-107, 308-520, 540; Page Smith, *Jefferson, A Revealing Biography*, (New York: American Heritage Publishing Company, 1976), pp. 206-211.

[91]Merlington, ed., *The Custer Story*, pp. 94, 104, 108, 146; Lowry, *The Story the Soldiers Wouldn't Tell*, pp. 154-155; Wert, *Custer*, pp. 106-107; Custer, *Tenting on the Plains*, p. 10.

[92]Lewis, *The Guns of Cedar Creek*, p. 86.

[93]Wert, *Custer*, p. 106; Quaife, ed., *My Life on the Plains*, pp. 299; Custer, *Tenting on the Plains*, p. 10.

[94]Quaife, ed., *My Life on the Plains*, p. 299.

[95]Ibid., pp. 237-238; Lewis, *The Guns of Cedar Creek*, p. 86.

[96]Merlington, ed., *The Custer Story*, p. 61; Lewis, The Guns of Cedar Creek, p. 86; Wert, Custer, p. 106; Adrain Jawort, "Did Custer Have a Cheyenne Mistress and Son? Native Oral History Says Yes," *Indian Country-Today*, February 1, 2017.

[97]Merlington, ed., *The Custer Story*, pp. 104, 131, 197; *Custer Centennial Issue, By Valor and Arms*, The Journal of American Military History, vol. 2, no. 2, p. 15; Jawort, "Did Custer Have a Cheyenne Mistress and Son? Native Oral History Says Yes," *Indian-Country-Today*, February 1, 2017.

[98]Wert, *Custer*, p. 107.

[99]Lewis, *The Guns of Cedar Creek*, p. 86.

[100]Ibid; Gordon-Reed, *The Hemingses of Monticello*, pp. 23-32, 516-518, 540-541, 550, 554-561; Jawort, "Did Custer Have A Cheyenne Mistress and Son? Native Oral History Says Yes," *Indian-Country Today*, February 1, 2017; Merington, ed., *The Custer Story*, pp. 94, 99, 104-105, 108, 120, 131, 134, 146, 197-198, 226; Wert, *Custer*, p. 107.

[101]Merington, ed., *The Custer Story*, pp. 94, 99, 104-105, 108, 120, 131, 134, 146, 197-198, 226; Wert, *Custer*, p. 107; Connell, *Son of the Morning Star*, p. 125.

[102]Merlington, ed., *The Custer Story*, p. 61.

[103]Wert, *Custer*, p. 107; Connell, *Son of the Morning Star*, p. 125.

[104]Connell, *Son of the Morning Star*, p. 125; Wert, *Custer*, p. 107; Jawort, "Did Custer Have a Cheyenne Mistress and Son? Native Oral History Says Yes," *Indian-Country Today*, February 1, 2017.

[105]Wert, *Custer*, 107; Connell, *Son of the Morning Star*, p. 125.

[106]Connell, *Son of the Morning Star*, p. 125.

[107]Ibid; Ladenheim, *Custer's Thorn*, pp. 3-4.

[108]Elise Lemire, *"Miscegenation," Making Race in America*, (Philadelphia: University of Pennsylvania Press, 2002), pp. 53-86; Connell, Son of the Morning Star, p. 125.

[109]Gordon-Reed, *The Hemingses of Monticello*, pp. 23-32, 285-286, 517-518; Andrew Burstein, *Jefferson's Secrets, Death and Desire at Monticello*, (New York: Perseus Books Group, 2005), p. 158; Richard M. Ketchum, *The Winter Soldiers, The Battles of Trenton and Princeton*, (New York: Henry Holt and Company,

1973), p. 19; Smith, Jefferson, p. 206; Ladenheim, *Custer's Thorn*, pp. 3-4.

[110]Wert, *Custer*, p. 107.

[111]Connell, *Son of the Morning Star*, p. 125.

[112]Ibid; Ladenheim, *Custer's Thorn*, pp. 3-4; Wert, *Custer*, p. 107.

[113]Connell, *Son of the Morning Star*, p. 125.

[114]Wert, *Custer*, p. 107; Gordon-Reed, *The Hemingses of Monticello*, pp. 23-32, 517-518; Burstein, *Jefferson's Secrets*, pp. 4, 157-160; Smith, *Jefferson*, pp. 206-207.

[115]Merington, ed., *The Custer Story*, pp. 61; Tucker, *Custer at Gettysburg*, pp. 299-402.

[116]Ladenheim, *Custer's Thorn*, pp. 131-132; Wert, *Custer*, pp. 106-107; Connell, *Son of the Morning Star*, p. 125.

[117]Merington, ed., *The Custer Story*, p. 168.

[118]Ibid., pp. 94, 104-105, 108, 120, 130, 132, 146, 198, 226.

[119]Connell, *Son of the Morning Star*, p. 125.

[120]Ibid.

[121]Ibid; Smith, *Jefferson*, pp. 206-207.

[122]Lowry, *The Story the Soldiers Wouldn't Tell*, pp. 154-155.

[123]Smith, *Jefferson*, p. 210; Wert, *Custer*, p. 107; Connell, *Son of the Morning Star*, p. 125.

[124]Wert, *Custer*, p. 107; Connell, *Son of the Morning Star*, p. 125.

[125]Merlington, ed., The Custer Story, p. 94.

[126]Ibid., p. 104.

[127]Ibid., p. 146.

[128]Ibid., p. 146; Blassingame, *The Slave Community*, pp. 41-42, 57-59, 75-76.

[129]Wert, *Custer*, pp. 211-212.

[130] Ibid., p. 212.

[131] Merlington, ed., *The Custer Story*, pp. 61, 226; Wert, Custer, pp. 211-212; Lowry, *The Story the Soldiers Wouldn't Tell*, pp. ix-27; Custer, *Tenting on the Plains*, pp. 159-167, 245-246.

[132] Merlington, ed., *The Custer Story*, p. 226

[133] Ibid.

[134] Merlington, ed., *The Custer Story*, p. 108.

[135] Ibid., 131.

[136] Ibid., pp. 133-134.

[137] Custer, *Tenting on the Plains*, p. 347.

[138] Merington, ed., *The Custer Story*, p. 198.

[139] Ibid., pp. 146, 198.

[140] Ibid., p. 61.

[141] Ibid., pp. 167-168.

[142] Merington, ed., *The Custer Story*, p. 209.

[143] Ibid. p. 226.

[144] Wert, *Custer*, p. 107; Connell, *Son of the Morning Star*, p. 125.

[145] Lewis, *The Guns of Cedar Creek*, p. 86; Merington, ed., *The Custer Story*, pp. 108, 131; Connell, *Son of the Morning Star*, p. 125; Michael Cottman, "Historians Uncover Slave Quarters of Sally Hemings at Thomas Jefferson's Monticello," NBC News, July 3, 2007.

[146] Merington, ed., *The Custer Story*, pp. 94, 209.

[147] Ibid., p. 132.

[148] Ibid., pp. 94, 104, 108, 120, 130, 132, 146, 198, 226; Wert, *Custer*, p. 107.

[149] Merington, ed., *The Custer Story*, pp. 177-178.

[150] Custer, *Tenting on the Plains*, p. 376.

[151] Ibid; Tucker, *Cathy Williams*, pp. 193-223.

[152]Merington, ed., *The Custer Story*, pp. 94, 104-105, 108, 120, 130, 132, 146, 198, 226; Custer, *Tenting on the Plains*, pp. 10, Wert, *Custer*, pp. 106-107.

www.ingramcontent.com/pod-product-compliance
Lightning Source LLC
Chambersburg PA
CBHW070750160726
48004CB00001B/133